BRITISH LABOUR STRUGGLES:
CONTEMPORARY PAMPHLETS 1727-1850

REBIRTH

OF

THE TRADE UNION MOVEMENT

Five Pamphlets

1838-1847

Arno Press

A New York Times Company/New York 1972

Reprint Edition 1972 by Arno Press Inc.

Reprinted from copies in the Kress Library
Graduate School of Business Administration,
Harvard University

BRITISH LABOUR STRUGGLES: CONTEMPORARY PAMPHLETS 1727-1850
ISBN for complete set: 0-405-04410-0

See last pages for complete listing.

Manufactured in the United States of America

Library of Congress Cataloging in Publication Data
Main entry under title:

Rebirth of the trade union movement.

    (British labour struggles:
contemporary pamphlets 1727-1850)
    CONTENTS: A brief treatise on the law of combina-
tion, by M. O'Donnell [first published 1838].--An
inquiry into the origin, progress, and results of the
strike of the operative cotton spinners of Preston,
by H. Ashworth [first published 1838].--Rules to be
observed by the members of the United Order of Smiths
[first published 1839]. [etc.]
    1. Trade-unions--Great Britain. I. Series.
HD6664.R38   331.89'2942   72-2539
ISBN 0-405-04431-3

Contents

A BRIEF TREATISE

ON THE

LAW OF COMBINATION,

ON UNLAWFUL SOCIETIES,

AND ON THE

ADMINISTRATION OF UNLAWFUL OATHS

IN WHICH

THE PRESENT STATE OF THE COMMON AND STATUTE LAW IN IRELAND
AFFECTING BOTH MASTER AND WORKMAN, IS FULLY EXPLAINED.

WITH AN APPENDIX,

CONTAINING THE 6TH GEO. 4TH, c. 129.

BY

MATTHEW O'DONNELL, ESQ.

BARRISTER AT LAW.

DUBLIN
HODGES AND SMITH, 21, COLLEGE-GREEN.

MDCCCXXXVIII.

Dublin: Printed by JOHN S. FOLDS, 5, Bachelor's-Walk.

PREFACE.

THERE are few subjects that have lately engaged more of the public attention than that of combination. How far the legislature ought to regulate or direct the disposal of combined labour or capital, must be a question of considerable interest to a commercial nation; great differences have prevailed—much angry discussion has been excited,—offences may sometimes have been committed from a misconception or from ignorance of the law, and it, therefore, appeared to be desirable that its present state should be clearly and exactly understood.

The writer of this treatise has attempted to effect this object. Should he be successful, and should the offender against the law abstain from its violation, from the knowledge that such a violation must injure his cause—some advantage may perhaps be thereby derived by the community.

As this little work has been principally intended for the use of unprofessional persons, the writer has endeavoured briefly and distinctly to digest and explain both the Common and Statute Law relating to Combination, to unlawful Societies, and the administration of unlawful Oaths, affecting master and workman, so as to be capable of being understood by every individual. But he has carefully abstained from giving any opinion upon the policy of the Law, as in such a compilation, it would be both uncalled for and impertinent.

It may be right to mention, that in compliance with the desire of some individuals, he would have willingly entered into a review of the Law, as it affects both master and workman generally, in relation to civil contracts and agreements; but he was deterred from so doing, from the belief that this compilation would thereby have become so enlarged, that its price would not render it generally accessible to the persons for whose use it was principally prepared—the Working Classes.

9, *Great Charles-street,*
February 24th, 1838.

TABLE OF CONTENTS.

ERRATA.

Page 1, note (°) after 3 S. T. add T. R ; for 2 Tea, A.D.B. read 2 Dea. A.B.

CHAPTER I.

OF THE OFFENCE OF COMBINATION AT
COMMON LAW.

THE spirit of the common law appears to have ever been opposed to every species of confederacy or combination injurious to private individuals, or prejudicial to the community: thus combinations, formed for the purpose of subverting public justice,[a] restraining public trade[b], injuring morality or public decency[c], or depreciating the reputation or profession of any member of society,[d] have been considered very grave offences. Such associations are included under the common name of conspiracy; and, as it is not intended to enter into the general law upon the latter subject, those peculiar instances of it shall alone be exemplified, which, being in restraint of public trade, are generally designated illegal combinations :—such

[a] *Hawkins' Pleas of the Crown, b.* 1, *ch.* 21, *Sect.* 15. *Joliffe's case,* 4 *T. R.* 285. *Mawbey's case,* 6 *T. R.* 619.
[b] *Eccles's case,* 1 *Leach* 274. *Turner's case,* 13 *East.* 228. *Levi v. Levi,* 6 *C. & P.* 240.
[c] *Lord Grey's case,* 3 *St.* 519. *Wakefield's case,* 2 *Tea. A.D.B.* 4.
[d] *Eccles's case, cited. Lee's case,* 2 *M'Nally, Evid.* 634.

B

combinations are supposed to restrain the freedom permitted to every person in the enjoyment of his occupation or profession, and to diminish the profit and advantage to be derived by the public from individual labor and exertion. What the common law deems to be combination with the evidence necessary for its proof, shall in this chapter be considered— the alterations or modifications by statute shall be subsequently explained. The administration of unlawful oaths—and associations, and confederacies, rendered illegal by statute, so far as they affect the relation of employers and workmen, shall also be considered.

Definition of Conspiracy. As illegal combination is but a species of the offence called conspiracy and included within it—its meaning may perhaps be most clearly understood by endeavouring to give a definition of the crime of conspiracy, and then referring to some cases which have been decided to be combinations prohibited by law.

Mr. *Sergeant Talfourd* [c] says, " that the offence of " conspiracy is more difficult to be ascertained pre-" cisely than any other for which an indictment lies ; " and is indeed rather to be considered as governed " by positive decisions than by any consistent and " intelligible principles of law. It consists, according " to all the authorities, not in the accomplishment of " any unlawful or injurious purpose, nor in any one " act moving towards that purpose ; but in the actual " concert and agreement of two or more persons, to " effect something which *being so concerted and agreed,*

[c] *Dickinson's Sessions by Talfourd.*

" the law regards as the object of an indictable
" conspiracy."

Mr. *Chitty* defines the offence of conspiracy to consist in " two or more combining together to execute
" some act for the purpose of injuring a third person
" or the public,[f] and

Bushe, C. J. defines it to be when " two or more
" persons confederate together for the effecting of an
" illegal purpose, or to effect a legal purpose by the
" use of unlawful means, even although such purpose
" should never be effected."[g]

It is laid down in a book of very great authority,
that all confederacies whatsoever wrongfully to prejudice a third person, are highly criminal at common
law,[h] and to constitute the offence of conspiracy
against the public, it is not necessary that it should
be prejudicial to the public in its aggregate capacity
or to *all* the King's subjects; but it is enough
if it be prejudicial to a particular class of those
subjects.[i]

The nature of a conspiracy or a combination
requires that more than one person should be engaged
in it; and in many cases even an agreement by two
or more to do a certain act has been considered the
subject of an indictment for a conspiracy, although
the same act, if done separately by each individual
without any concert, would not be indictable or
punishable.

Necessary that more than one person should be engaged in it.

---

[f] *Burn's Justice, by Chitty, vol.* 1, 816.
[g] *The King* v. *Forbes and Others, Green's Report,* 349.
[h] 1 *Hawk P. C. ch.* 72, *sec.* 2.
[i] *Per Bayley, J.* 3 *Mau. & Scl.* 75.

4

Combination of workmen not to work under certain wages.

Thus in the case of the *King* v. *the Journeymen Tailors of Cambridge*,[j] it was decided that a conspiracy among journeymen to refuse to work under certain wages was an indictable offence, although the matter about which they conspired might have been lawful for any of them to do if they had not conspired to do it ; thus also, if several journeymen meet for the purpose of raising their wages, by the common law it was illegal, and the parties might be indicted for a conspiracy, although each might insist on raising his wages if he could ;[k] nor was it necessary in the above cases to prove that the journeymen succeeded in their object, viz.—raising their wages, as the combining together or the unlawful agreement, although nothing be done in the prosecution of it is the *gist*, or in other words, what constitutes the offence ;[l] but now workmen may combine under certain restrictions to regulate their wages, (*see next Chapter*).

To injure a third person in his trade.

When several persons combine together to impoverish a third party in his trade even by indirect means—it is an illegal combination and conspiracy, as in the case of the *King* v. *Cope and others*,[m] where a husband and wife and servants were indicted for a conspiracy to ruin the trade of the prosecutor, who was the King's card maker—and the evidence against them was, that they at several times had given money to the prosecutor's apprentices to put grease into the paste which had spoiled the cards; and also in the

[j] 8 *Mod.* 11.
[k] *Rex* v. *Mawbey and others*, 6 *T. Rep.* 637. 8 *Mod.* 320.
[l] *The King* v. *Spragg and others*, 2 *Burr* 993.　　[m] 1 *Stra.* 144.

case of the *King* v. *Eccles*[n] *and others*, where the defendants were found guilty, and adjudged six months' imprisonment, for combining together by indirect means, to prevent one H. B. from exercising the trade of a tailor, and, as such a combination was considered to be in restraint of public trade, it was deemed to be clearly indictable, although the means used to prevent H. B. were not stated.

A combination to prevent the workmen of an employer from continuing their work, is by the common law indictable, and will be supported by the evidence of a conspiracy to prevent *any* workman from continuing his work,[o] and a combination of workmen, for the purpose of dictating to masters what workmen they should employ, or to compel masters to discharge certain workmen, is indictable ;[p] so also it is indictable for workmen to refuse to work, and to absent themselves from their employer for the purpose of procuring the discharge of a workman, because he declined paying a fine imposed for the violation of certain rules alleged to be made for the regulation of the trade;[q] so a conspiracy by workmen to prevent their masters from taking *any* apprentices ; or to prevent them from taking or instructing more than a certain number they then had, is indictable;[r] so also, a combination amongst workmen to turn out from their employment until

To prevent workmen or any workman from continuing their or his work.

To dictate to masters what workmen they should employ.

To absent themselves for the purpose of obtaining the discharge of a workman.

To prevent masters from taking any apprentices, or more than a certain number.

---

[n] 1 *Leach.* 274.   [o] *Rex* v. *Byerdike*, 1 *Moo. & Rob.* 179.
[p] *Ibid.* 180.   [q] *Rex* v. *Salter*, 5 *Esp.* 124.
[r] 2 *Stark. N. P. C.* 489. As in the case of the *King* v. *Ferguson* and *Edge*, where the defendants being journeymen, in the trade of engravers, combined to prevent their employer from retaining and taking into their employment *any* person as an apprentice ; they

certain workmen and apprentices were dismissed. *See note* [r].

Combination of masters.

The combinations of masters or employers in restraint of trade, are also considered by the common law illegal and indictable—thus, if the masters of workmen combine together to lower the rate of wages, they also were liable to be punished for a conspiracy, [*] *(but see next chapter)*; so also, although they may sell their articles of trade at such prices as they individually may please, yet if they confederate

were also charged with combining to leave their employment until certain workmen and apprentices were dismissed.

It appeared that upon the prosecutors taking into their employment a young man named Green as an apprentice, the defendants, together with a number of journeymen, declared to the prosecutors that they would not stand it, and after consultation left their work, and that *Edge's* agreement was given up to him, and he went away. The rest of the workmen were conciliated for a time, by the prosecutors agreeing to relinquish *Green* as an apprentice. Sometime afterwards *Ferguson* and the other workmen again turned out, upon the prosecutors taking into their service another apprentice of the name of *Merone.* At the time of turn out, the prosecutors had in their employment *sixteen* journeymen and *eight* apprentices, and it appeared upon the cross-examination of one of the prosecutors, that the objection which had been made by the defendants and their associates did not apply to the *eight* apprentices which the prosecutors then had in their employment, but that they objected to the prosecutors taking a greater number of apprentices than *half* the number of journeymen. Although it was objected upon this evidence, that it varied from the charge which alleged, generally, a conspiracy to prevent the masters from taking into their employment *any* apprentices; whereas it appeared that they only objected to the taking of any *more* apprentices, or a *number exceeding half the number of journeymen*, yet it was decided that the evidence sufficiently supported the indictment, and the defendants were found *guilty*, and received sentence of fine and imprisonment.

[s] *Hammond's case*, 2 *Esp. N.P. C.* 720.

and agree not to sell them under certain prices, they are guilty of a conspiracy;[t] and in fact all combinations and confederacies, either of employers or workmen, for the purpose of raising or lowering the rate of wages, limiting the time of labour, or the number of apprentices, or for any other purpose interfering with that freedom permitted by law to every individual in his trade or profession, or injurious to the public, or in restraint of trade, are by the common law indictable and punishable as conspiracies. In the next chapter it shall be considered how far the common law has been altered or modified by statute. Previous to the explanation of the evidence necessary to prove a combination or conspiracy, it is proper to mention that although the nature of the offence requires that more than one person should be concerned in its commission, yet where two persons are indicted for a conspiracy, one of them may be convicted, although the other, who has pleaded and is alive, has not been tried, and though it is possible he may be afterwards acquitted;[u] so also one conspirator may be tried singly, and rightly convicted alone, when the other conspirators charged by the indictment shall not have appeared, or shall have escaped, or died before the time of trial, or before the finding of the bill.[v]

Summary of combinations illegal at common law.

It has been a question of great difficulty, whether it is competent for the prosecutor to shew, in the first instance, the existence of a conspiracy or combination

Of the evidence.

[t] *Per Lord Mansfield, Eccles's case* 1. *Leach.* 276.

[u] *Cooke's case,* 5 B. & C. 538. 7 D. & R. 673.

[v] *R. v. Kinnersley,* 1 *Stra.* 193. *R. v. Nichols,* 2 *Stra.* 1227.

amongst other persons, than, the defendants, previous to the proof of the knowledge or concurrence of those defendants; and it appears, that in general, such evidence may be admitted—thus, Mr. *Justice Buller* thought that evidence might be, in the first instance, given of a conspiracy without proof of the defendants participation in it,[w] and *Eyre*, C. J. said that in the case of a conspiracy general evidence of the thing conspired is received, and then the party before the Court is to be affected for his share of it.[x] Thus, upon a prosecution for a conspiracy to raise the rate of wages, proof was given of an association of persons for that purpose, of meetings, of rules being printed, and of mutual subscriptions.[y] It was objected, that evidence could not be given of those facts, without first bringing them home to the defendants, and making them parties to the illegal combination; but Lord *Kenyon* permitted a person who was a member of the society, to prove the printed rules and regulations, and that he and others acted under them, previous to the proof that the defendants were members of the same society, and equally involved in it; but added that it would not be evidence to affect the defendants until they were made parties to the same conspiracy. In many of the state trials, evidence has been given of a general conspiracy, before any proof of the part the accused parties may have taken in it,[z] and in the *Queen's case*,[a]

---

[w] *Hardy's case.—Gurney's Edit. St. Tr. Vol.* 1. *p.* 360.

[x] *Ibid.*   [y] *Hammond's case,* 2 *Esp. N.P.C.* 720.

[z] *Lord Russell's case,* 9 *St. Trials,* 578. *Lord Lovatt's case,* 18 *St. Trials,* 530. *Horne Tooke's case,* 25 *St. Trials,* 1.

[a] 2 *Brod. & Bing.* 310.

the rule has been finally settled, that on the prosecution of a crime to be proved by conspiracy, general
evidence of an existing conspiracy may, in the first
instance, be received, as a preliminary step to
that more particular evidence, by which it is to be
shewn that the individual defendants were guilty
participators in such conspiracy ; and it follows, from
the above rule, that in an indictment for an illegal
combination or confederacy, the existence of such a
combination may be given in evidence previous to
the proof of the participation of the defendants
in it.

The existence of an illegal combination may be
proved either directly, as by proof of meeting and
consulting for the illegal purpose, submitting to
certain rules, and subscribing to a common fund,
or more usually by circumstantial evidence from the
very nature of the offence, *Bushe, C. J.* in the case
of the *King* v. *Forbes,* and others,[b] says, " that the
" evidence of a conspiracy must from the nature
" of the thing, be in most cases circumstantial, indeed
" must be always so, except in those cases where
" by accident the conspirators have been overheard,
" or where an accomplice in the guilt comes forward
" to betray his associates."

How it is to be proved.

By circumstantial evidence is meant such evidence
as will afford a fair and reasonable presumption of
the offence to be tried, and it belongs alone to the
jury to determine, (under the direction of the Judge,)
whether the force and effect of the circumstances
proved, are sufficiently satisfactory and convincing

*Circumstan-
tial evidence,
what.*

to warrant them in finding the guilt or innocence of the prisoner ;[c] and " in drawing an inference or con-
" clusion from facts proved, regard must be had to the
" nature of the particular case, and the facility that
" appears to be afforded, either of explanation or
" contradiction. No person is required to explain
" or contradict, until enough has been proved to
" warrant a reasonable and just conclusion against
" him, in the absence of explanation or contradic-
" tion ; but when such proof has been given, and
" the nature of the case is such as to admit of expla-
" nation or contradiction, if the conclusion to which
" the proof tends be untrue, and the accused offers
" no explanation or contradiction, human reason
" cannot do otherwise than adopt the conclusion to
" which the proof tends."[d]   Those observations of
Lord *Tenterden*, are forcibly applicable to the offence
of illegal combination, which, as already has been
observed, must generally depend upon circumstantial
evidence ; thus evidence of a previous combination
may be presumed, from the defendant and other
persons concerting or concurring together at the
same time, and for the same object, and the greater
the similarity or coincidence, in the means employed,
to effect the object, the stronger will be the evidence
of a previous combination and agreement between
the parties :[e] thus, in the case of the *King* v. *Cope*
and others, already referred to,[f] where a husband,
wife, and servants were indicted for conspiring to

Indictment for ruining the trade of card maker.

[c] *2 H. Bla.* 297.
[d] *By Lord Tenterden in the case of the King* v. *Sir F. Burdett.* 4 *Bar. & Ald.* 161.
[e] 1 *East. P. C.* 96, 97.   [f] *Ante page* 4.

ruin the trade of a card maker, by giving money to the apprentice for putting grease into the paste, which spoiled the cards, although there was no evidence given, that more than one of the defendants was ever present, (though all had given money in their turns,) and it was objected that this could not be a conspiracy, for two men might do the same thing without any previous communication, yet, the defendants being of one family, and concerned in the trade of card making, it was decided that it amounted to evidence of a previous combination and conspiracy[g] ; and there are numerous cases to which, in a treatise of this kind, it is not necessary particularly to refer, that clearly establish the principle, that in prosecutions for every species of conspiracy, the fact of the conspiracy may be presumed from even collateral facts and circumstances, and sometimes from cumulative or repeated instances of acts, similar to that which is the immediate object of the indictment.[h]

Having proved the existence of the combination and the defendant's connexion with it—*the acts or declarations of any individual member of the same combination in pursuance of the common object of such combination will be admitted as evidence against all the defendants.* The rule upon this subject is fully established and is of the greatest importance, and well deserves the serious consideration of every member of an illegal combination or society. A very distinguished writer upon the law of evidence, [i] says ;

Of the evidence. Acts or declarations of one, evidence against another

[g] *And see Lee's case, M·Nally on Evid. 634.*
[h] *Rex* v. *Parsons and others,* 1 *Black,* 392. *Rex* v. *Roberts and others,* 1 *Campb.* 399.
[i] *Mr. Philips, 7th Edit.* 1 *Vol.* 94.

12

" In prosecutions for conspiracies, it is an established
" rule that, when several persons are proved to have
" combined together for the same illegal purpose, any
" act done by one of the party, in pursuance of the
" original concerted plan and with reference to the
" common object is, in contemplation of the law, as
" well as in sound reason, the act of the whole party :
" and therefore, the proof of such act will be evidence
" against any of the others who were engaged in the
" same general conspiracy, without regard to the
" question whether the prisoner is proved to have
" been concerned in that particular transaction."
And in the case of the *King* v. *Watson*,[j] *Mr. Justice Bayley* is reported to have said that " He who
" plans a thing, or who devises the means by which
" it is to be effected, or draws in others to cooperate
" or does any other act preparatory to the execution
" of the thing proposed, is as much a principal as he
" who executes that thing : and provided a man once
" comes into the common purpose and design, every
" previous act done with a view to that purpose and
" design, and every subsequent act is as much his
" act as if he had done it himself."
And the same rule, subject to the same limitations,
must apply to the *declarations* of persons combining
as well as to their acts. Mr. Philips says " That
" any declarations made by one of the party, in pur-
" suance of the common object of the conspiracy, are
" evidence against the rest of the party who are as

[j] *Watson's case*, 32 *How. St. Trials*, 7. *And see Bedford*
v. *Birley*, 3 *Stark, N. P. C.* 85.

" much responsible for all that has been said or done
" by their associates in carrying into effect the con-
" certed plan as if it had been *pronounced by their*
" *own voice, or executed by their own hand.* All con-
" sultations, therefore, carried on by one conspirator,
" relative to the general design, and all conversations
" in his presence, are evidence against another,
" although absent, but the effect of such conversation
" will depend upon a variety of circumstances, such
" as whether he was attending to the conversation—
" whether he approved or disapproved ; but still such
" conversations are admissible in evidence."[k] And it
makes no difference as to the admissibility of this
evidence, whether the other combinators be indicted
or not, tried or not, for making them defendants
would give no additional strength to their declarations
against others, nor is it material what the nature of
the conspiracy is, provided the offence involve a conspiracy. Persons may even be connected by evidence
with a conspiracy which in its original formation was
remote in time as well as place from the particular
acts imputed to the defendants. Thus in the case of
Hammond and *Webb*[l], already referred to,—the indictment charged defendants, who were journeymen shoemakers, with a combination to raise their wages ; and
evidence was offered, on the part of the prosecution,
of a plan for combination among the journeymen
shoemakers, formed and printed several years before,
regulating their meetings, subscriptions, and other
matters, for their mutual government, in forwarding

[k] *Phil. on Evidence*, 96.   24 *How. St. Trials*, 704.
[l] *Ante page* 8.

their designs ; the evidence being objected to by counsel for defendants, *Lord Kenyon said* that if a general conspiracy existed, general evidence might be given of its nature, and the conduct of its members, so as to implicate men who stood charged with acting upon the terms of it, *years after those terms had been established,* and who *might reside at a great distance, from the place where the general plan was carried on.*

And in the case of *Salter* and *Another,*[m] who were indicted for a conspiracy to compel a master hat-maker, to discharge the prosecutor because he did not pay a fine, for having broken the rules entered into by them and others, for the regulation of journeymen it was decided by *Hotham B.*—That as the prosecutor had proved, that at a meeting of the defendants and several other persons, the fine was demanded; it was competent for him to prove the declarations of the persons at such meeting : although it was objected that the criminality of the defendants could only be inferred from their own declarations. But what one of the party may have said not in furtherance of the plot, but as a mere relation of some past transaction, or as to the share which some other persons have had in the execution of the common design, cannot, it appears, be admitted as evidence to affect other persons.[n] It appears therefore, clearly to be decided, that in all illegal combinations and conspiracies formed for the purpose of raising or diminishing wages—raising the price of commodities—limiting the number

[m] *Ante page 5.*
[n] 2 *Esp. N. P. R.* 718. *Phil. on Evidence,* 97, 98. *Rex.* v. *Hardy.*—*Howell's St. Trials,* 452, 475.

of apprentices—or for any other purpose interfering with the freedom permitted by law to every individual to enjoy in his trade or occupation—every member of such a combination is not alone responsible for his own acts and expressions, but also for the acts and expressions of every other member of the same society, even if performed or spoken at distant places and at different times, in prosecution of the common object or design—and although it should appear that the accused member had no communication whatsoever, or was perfectly unknown to the individual whose acts or declarations may be given in evidence against him. This is a peculiarity of the law of conspiracy—it may sometimes operate with much severity, but yet every individual should pause before he enrolled himself in any club or association which might afterwards involve him in so very serious a responsibility.

The nature of an illegal combination at common law has now been explained with the evidence necessary for its support, and it remains but to add, that if upon a trial, such evidence should be given as will afford a reasonable presumption of the guilt of the persons charged, the jury, under the direction of the court, ought to find a verdict of guilty; if, on the other side, the combination or conspiracy should not be properly established, or there should be a reasonable doubt of the connexion of the defendants with it, they are of course entitled to the benefit of that doubt, and ought to be acquitted. The offence is Punishment. what is termed a misdemeanor at common law, and punished by fine and imprisonment, according to the discretion of the court. In the next chapter shall be considered the offences created, and the alterations or modifications of the common law introduced by statute.

Before the conclusion of this chapter, it is right to state, that in case two or more persons should be indicted for belonging to any illegal association or conspiracy—great difficulty must be felt in the examination of any member of the same illegal body as a witness in favor of the prisoners : for if it should appear from the evidence, that the witness belonged to the same confederacy, he will immediately incur the very great hazard of being removed from the witness-box to the dock, to be subsequently tried for a similar offence.

CHAPTER II.

OF THE STATUTE LAW.

ALTHOUGH by the common law protection was intended to be afforded to every man in the employment
of labor or the investment of capital, yet in many
cases it was supposed to be unable to suppress that
spirit of combination and confederacy which appears
to have existed from a very early period—hence it
was that the legislature thought it necessary, from
time to time, to enact several statutes[a] for the suppression of combination both of employers and
workmen in different trades and manufactures—many
of which statutes were most severe in the punishment
attached to the offence.[b] The several statutes and
parts of statutes relating to combination were repealed by the 5th *Geo. 4th, c.* 95, and provision was
made for protecting the free employment of capital,
and for rendering certain combinations and confederacies legal, provided they did not interfere with
such freedom by means of violence, threats, or in-

[a] They are enumerated in the 1st Section of 6th Geo. 4th, c. 129.
See Appendix.

[b] As the 3rd *Henry* 6th, c. 1, passed in 1425, which made it a
felony for masons to confederate together to advance wages above the
statutory rate.

C

18

By the 5th Geo. 4th, c. 95, combinations of workmen rendered legal. timidation. Thus the second section of the latter statute[c] legalised every combination of workmen formed for the purpose of obtaining an advance or fixing the rate of wages,—lessening, altering, or regulating the time or quantity of work, inducing others to depart from the employment, or return their work unfinished, —refusing to enter into work or employment, or combinations for the purpose of regulating the management of any trade or business;—and the persons engaged in such combinations were expressly exempted from any prosecution to which they otherwise might be liable by the common or statute law.

Combinations of Masters. The masters or employers of workmen were likewise exempted by this statute from every species of prosecution for combining to lower the rate of wages— increase or alter the hours of working—increase the quantity of work—or otherwise regulate the mode of conducting their respective trades and manufactures.[d]

Offences created by this Statute. But by the 5th section of the same statute,[e] if any person should, by violence, or by threats, or by intimidation, wilfully and maliciously force another to depart from his work or return his work before it had been finished ; or should, by violence, or by threats, or by intimidation, wilfully and maliciously spoil or destroy any machinery, or should, by any or either of the above means, prevent any person from accepting work or employment; or if any person should use violence, threats, or intimidation to another for not conforming to certain rules or regulations, made for the purpose

[c] See the 2nd section of 5th *Geo.* 4th, *c.* 95.
[d] See 3rd section of 5th *Geo.* 4th, *c.* 95.
[e] See 5th section same statute.

of obtaining an advance of wages, altering the hours, or decreasing the quantity of work,—regulating the mode of carrying on any manufacture, or made for the purpose of forcing employers to make alterations in the mode of carrying on their respective trades and manufactures—every person or persons so offending, his or their aiders and abettors were upon conviction subject to an imprisonment of two calendar months, and might be kept to hard labor.[f] And by the 6th *section*, persons combining to effect by violence, or by threats, or by intimidation, any of the purposes above mentioned, became subject, upon conviction, to the same punishment.[g] By the extracts from the above statute, it will be perceived that the object of the legislature in its enactment was,—to render perfectly legal every species of combination, provided the members of such a combination did not by violence or intimidation interfere with that right which every man is supposed to possess over his own industry, skill, and capital.

Immediately after the enactment of the last mentioned statute, combinations of workmen increased to an alarming extent in different parts of the United Kingdom—many breaches of the peace and other disturbances occurred, especially in Scotland, in consequence of the disputes between masters and workmen.[h] The common and statute law relating to combination were repealed—the provisions of the 5th

---

[f] See 5th Section of same Statute.
[g] See 6th Section of same Statute.
[h] See Hansard's Par. Debates, vol. 13 (New Series) 1400, 1455, 1462.

Repeal of the *Geo. 4th* were found ineffectual, and the legislature
5th *Geo.* 4th,
c. 95. therefore, and in consequence of numerous petitions
having been presented to Parliament from many ma-
nufacturing districts, was compelled, in the year subsequent to its passing, to repeal the 5*th Geo.* 4*th, c.*
95. The act by which the last mentioned statute
was repealed is the 6*th Geo.* 4*th, c.* 129. It became
a law on the 6*th of July*, 1825.

The 6th *Geo.* The 6*th Geo.* 4*th, c.* 129,[i] which has been most
4th, *c.* 129.
aptly designated " the great charter of the working
classes," is the statute which at present regulates the
relation of employer and workman in every part of
the United Kingdom ; as it is an act which exactly defines the rights and liabilities both of the
employer and employed—it is intended in this chapter
to endeavour clearly and distinctly to point out and
explain both the offences which it creates and the
privileges it bestows—those offences and privileges
shall be classified ; and as the object of the publication
of this little work was not so much that it should be
read by professional persons, as that it should be
understood by those engaged in trade and manufactures,—the important sections of the statute shall be
fully detailed—the writer preferring even the risk of
being supposed tedious, to the danger of leaving any
portion of it ambiguous or unexplained.

The 6th *Geo.* The Act of the 6th *Geo.* 4*th,* appears to have
4th, *c.* 129—
its object. followed a mediate course between the extreme restriction of the common law, and the unlimited freedom
of the repealed statute. Whilst it recognizes the

---

[i] Commonly called " Hume's Act." It was principally owing to
Mr. Hume's exertions that the Combination Statutes were repealed.
See Han. Par. Deb. v. 10, 141 ; v. 11, 811.

right of every man to exercise the faculties of his
mind, or to dispose of the powers of his body, in the
manner he may deem most conducive to his advantage,
—yet it permits several persons, peaceably and voluntarily, to combine for the purpose of affixing a price
on labor, provided such a combination be within the
restrictions of its 4th and 5th sections; with this
exception—it has restored the common law; and
therefore, every species of confederacy, both of the
employer and the employed, unless protected within
the 4th and 5th sections of the statute, which shall be
subsequently detailed, must be governed by the
rules and decisions that have been already explained
in the preceding chapter.

- The first section of the 6th *Geo.* 4th, after reciting Its first section.
that the provisions of the 5th *Geo.* 4th, *c.* 95, were
not found effectual—that certain combinations were
injurious to trade and commerce, dangerous to the
tranquillity of the country, and especially prejudicial
to the interests of all engaged in them—states it to
be expedient to make further provision, as well for
the security and personal freedom of individual workmen in the disposal of their skill and labor, as for the
security of the property and persons of masters and
employers ; and for this purpose it repeals the latter
statute.

The second section of the statute repeals a great 2nd Section
number of statutes and portions of statutes relating statutes relating
to combination both of masters and workmen, passed to combination.
by the legislatures of England, Ireland, and Scotland, at different periods of time.

See the 4th and 5th Sections of the 6th Geo. 4th, c. 129, *post.*

The statutes or parts of statutes repealed, amount
in number to thirty-three, and form a successive series
from the remote period of the 33d year of Edward
the 1st to the 57th of George the 3rd—fourteen related exclusively to Ireland, and commenced
with the 33d Hen. 8th, s. 1. c. 9. Such of them as
relate to Great Britain exclusively, it is unnecessary
to enumerate. Those that immediately affected Ireland, were the 33d of Henry the 8th, s. 1. c. 9 ; 3d
Geo. 2nd, c. 14 ; 17th Geo. 2nd, c. 8 ; 3rd Geo. 3rd,
c. 17 ; 3rd Geo. 3rd, c. 34 ; 11th and 12th Geo. 3rd,
c. 18 ; 11th and 12th Geo. 3rd, c. 33 ; 19th and 20th
Geo. 3rd, c. 19 ; 19th and 20th Geo. 3rd, c. 24 ; 19th
and 20th Geo. 3rd, c. 36 ; 25th Geo. 3rd, c. 48 ; 43rd
Geo. 3rd. c. 86 ; 47th Geo. 3rd, s. 1. c. 43 ; and the
47th Geo. 3rd, c. 122.[k] The 2nd section of the 6th
Geo. 4th, after having enumerated and repealed those
statutes or parts of statutes, further repeals all enactments in any other statutes or acts, which, immediately before the passing of the 5th Geo. 4th, c. 95,
were in force throughout, or in any part of the united
kingdom, relative to combinations to obtain an advance
of wages, or to lessen or alter the hours or duration
of the time of working or the quantity of work—or
to regulate or control the mode of carrying on any
manufacture, trade, or business, or the management
thereof—or relative to combinations to lower the rate
of wages, or to increase or alter the hours or duration
of the time of working, or to increase the quantity of
work—or to regulate or control the mode of carrying

[k] The 29th Geo. 2nd, c. 12, made perpetual by 1st Geo. 3rd,
c.17, sec. 15, for punishing combination in Collieries and other mine
works in Ireland, is not repealed by the 6th Geo. 4th, c. 129.

23

on any manufacture, trade or business, or the management thereof—or relative to fixing the amount of the wages of labor, or relative to the obliging workmen not hired, to enter into work ;—and it further repeals every enactment enforcing or extending the application of any of the several enactments so repealed, except only so far as the same or any of them may have repealed any former act or enactment.

It is not to be supposed that by the repeal of those several enactments, combination is no longer an offence;—the offences created by those repealed statutes are removed, but the common law is not thereby affected,—and if, therefore, persons should illegally combine, although not liable to the statutory punishment, yet, they may still be indicted and convicted by the common law.[1] *The repeal of those statutes does not affect the common law.*

The offences prohibited as well as the privileges permitted by the 6th Geo. 4th, c. 129, shall now be considered.

The offences prohibited, consisting of a great variety that are enumerated in the 3rd section of the statute, may be reduced to three general heads :—First, offences to the person or property of the workman exclusively. Secondly, offences to the person or property of the master exclusively. Thirdly, offences to the person or property of a third party, which may include both master and workman as well as other individuals. *Of the offences prohibited by the 6th Geo. 4th.*

The means by which offences prohibited by the 3rd section may be committed, are, 1st, Violence to the person. 2nd, Violence to the property. 3rd, Threats. 4th, Intimidation. 5th, Molesting another person. 6th, In any way obstructing another. *The mode of commission.*

---

[1] See *Rex* v. *Byerdike,* 1 *Moo. & Rob.* 179.

Definition of workman.

Previous to the specification of the offences, it is necessary to state, that by the word workman is meant, any journeyman, manufacturer, workman, or other person hired or employed, or accustomed to be hired or employed, or accustomed to accept work or employment in any manufacture, trade, or business.

The offences to the person or property of the workman exclusively shall, in the first place, be specified —they are reduced to eight classes—the first four of which relate to hired workmen, the remainder to workmen not hired or employed.

Of the offences to workmen.

The offences to the person or property of the workman, prohibited by the 3d section, are—

[n] 1st. To *force any workman to depart* from his hiring, or employment, or work.

2nd. To *endeavour to force any workman to depart* from his hiring, or his employment or work.

3rd. To *force any workman to return his work* before the same should be finished.

4th. To *endeavour to force any workman to return his work* before the same should be finished.

5th. To *prevent* any workman not hired or employed *from hiring himself* to any person or persons.

6th. To *endeavour to prevent* any workman, not hired or employed *from hiring himself* to any person or persons.

7th. To *prevent any workman* not hired or employed from *accepting* work or employment from any person or persons.

8th. To *endeavour to prevent any workman* not hired or employed, from *accepting* work or employment from any person or persons.

[n] See 3rd section of 6th Geo. 4th, c. 129.

The offences to the person or property of the master exclusively, by which is meant " any manufacturer or other person carrying on any trade or business," may be reduced to the eight following classes :— Of offences to the master.

1st. To *force any master to make any alteration* in his mode of regulating, or managing, or conducting, or carrying on his manufacture, or his trade or business.

2nd. To *endeavour to force any master to make any alteration* in his mode of regulating, or managing, or conducting, or carrying on his manufacture, or trade, or business.

3rd. To *force* any master to *limit the number of his apprentices.*

4th. To *endeavour to force* any master to *limit the number of his apprentices.*

5th. To *force* any master to *limit the number of his journeymen, workmen, or servants.*

6th. To *endeavour to force* any master to *limit the number of his journeymen, workmen, or servants.*

7th. To *force* any master to *limit the description of his journeymen, workmen or servants.*

8th. To *endeavour to force* any master to *limit the description of his journeymen, workmen, or servants.*

The third and remaining species of offences within the third section of the statute, shall now be detailed :—namely, those offences to a third party, which may include both master and workman, and are reduced to the following eighteen classes. The part of the section now to be considered appears to be particularly directed against these offences, which may arise, or are connected with certain clubs and associations, both of employers and workmen, formed for the purpose of fixing the rate of wages, or regu- Of offences to a third person, which may include both master and workman.

lating the management of trade. They shall now be enumerated—

1st. It is criminal for any person to use or employ violence to the person or to the property of another, or to use or employ threats or intimidation, or to molest or in any way obstruct another, for the purpose of *forcing, or for the purpose of inducing* such person to belong to *any club or association.*

2nd. Or for the purpose of forcing or inducing such person to *contribute to any common fund.*

3rd. Or for the purpose of forcing or inducing such person to *pay any fine or penalty.*

4th. It is criminal for any person to use or employ to the person or property of another any or either of the above means, *on account of such other person not belonging* to any particular club or association.

5th. Or on account of such other person not *having contributed to any common fund.*

6th. Or on account of such other person *having refused* to contribute to any common fund.

7th. Or on account of such other person *not having contributed to pay any fine or penalty.*

8th. Or on account of such other person *having refused to pay* any fine or penalty.

9th. Or on account of such other person *not having complied with any* rules or orders or resolutions or regulations made to obtain an advance of wages.

10th. Or on account of such other person *refusing to comply* with any rules or orders or resolutions or regulations made to obtain an advance of wages.

11th. Or on account of such other person not having complied with any rules or orders or resolutions or regulations *made to reduce the rate of wages.*

12th. Or on account of such other person *refusing to comply* with any rules or orders or resolutions or regulations made to reduce the rate of wages.

13th. Or on account of such other person *not having complied* with any rules or orders or resolutions or regulations made to *lessen or alter the hours of working.*

14th. Or on account of such other person *refusing to comply* with any rules or orders or resolutions or regulations made to lessen or alter the hours of working.

15th. Or on account of such other person *not having complied* with any rules or orders or resolutions or regulations made to *decrease or alter the quantity of work.*

16th. Or on account of such other person *refusing to comply* with any rules or orders or resolutions or regulations made to decrease or alter the quantity of work.

17th. Or on account of such other person *not having complied* with any rules or orders or resolutions or regulations made to regulate the mode of carrying on any manufacture, trade or business—or made to regulate the management thereof.

18th. Or on account of such other person *refusing to comply* with any rules or orders or resolutions or regulations made to regulate the mode of carrying on any manufacture, trade, or business—or made to regulate the management thereof.

The entire of the several offences created by the third section of the statute have now been enumerated; and it is only necessary again to remind the reader, that any or either of them may be committed by violences to person or to property, by threats, by intimidation, by molesting or in any manner obstructing another.

Persons aiding or abetting equally liable. And the person who actually commits either of the several offences prohibited by the statute, is not alone liable; but every individual who aids, abets, or assists therein is rendered equally guilty as the principal offender, and may be convicted and punished accordingly.[n] Those several offences created by this section of the statute could not be punished as illegal combination by the common law, inasmuch as it is essentially necessary to constitute such an illegal combination, that two or more persons should participate and be engaged in the commission of the offence.

Mode of investigation. With respect to the mode of investigating the offences prohibited by this statute, the 7th section of the statute directs that:—[o] Upon complaint or information upon oath, of any of the above offences, having been committed within six calendar months previous to such complaint or information, and within his jurisdiction, a Justice of the Peace may summon the person charged with the offence to appear before two Justices, at a certain time and place—or in default of appearance and upon proof of due service of the summons, the Justices may issue a warrant for the apprehension of the offender;—or the Justices may, if they so think fit, issue a warrant in the first instance, and upon the appearance of the person charged, may proceed to hear and determine the case—and for that purpose may compel one offender to be a witness against another, provided such witness be indemnified from any prosecution, for offending in any matter relative to which he may be called on to give evidence;[p] the Justices may also summon witnesses, and in case any witness should

[n] See the 3d Section of the Statute.

[o] See 7th section.　　　　[p] See 6th section.

not appear, or should not submit to be examined, they may commit him to prison for three calendar months, or until such witness shall submit to be examined. The punishment attached to any of the se- Punishment. veral offences created by this statute is three calendar months' imprisonment, with or without hard labour, as the court may deem expedient,—but the person convicted may appeal to the next general quarter sessions of the peace having jurisdiction where the offence was committed,—upon entering into a recognizance to prosecute the appeal with effect.[q]

No master, in any trade or manufacture, can act as No master can act as Justice of the Peace in or concerning any offence Justice. alleged to have been committed under this statute.[r]

With respect to the evidence necessary to support a Of the evidence. conviction under this statute, dependant as it is upon a variety of circumstances, it is extremely difficult to lay down any general rule upon the subject. The words of the statute are very vague and indefinite, and perhaps designedly made so, in order to meet the many modes of impeding or interfering with that freedom of action which the law is desirous to protect in both master and workman. Although, to violate the provisions of the statute, it is not generally necessary that the object sought to be attained, should be effected,—as in many instances, even the endeavour or attempt is criminal, and it is almost impossible to state what may not be deemed molestation or obstruction—yet, it is therefore the more expedient, that the testimony should be clear, consistent, and satisfactory. Each case must depend upon its own circumstances—what may amount to molestation or

[q] See section 12.   [r] See section 13.

obstruction in one, may be perfectly harmless in another,—and if it should appear that a complainant, not impelled by a mere timid imagination, or by jealousy, hatred or revenge, clearly proves that he is impeded or obstructed in his employment or the mode of conducting his trade or business,—an offence is committed against the third section of this statute.

Lawful associations.

Having now endeavoured to classify the different offences against the third section of the 6th Geo. 4th, with the nature of the evidence ; the associations and agreements, both of workmen and masters, made lawful by this statute, shall now be specified, and the alterations thereby introduced into the common law shall then be explained—such combinations may be reduced to two general heads—first, those of workmen and others—second, those of masters and others.

By the fourth section of the 6th Geo. 4th, c. 129, the following meetings and agreements of workmen and other persons are rendered lawful, and the persons present at such meeting or entering into such agreements are exempted from any kind of punishment or penalty or prosecution.

Meetings of workmen.

With respect to meetings of workmen and other persons :—

1st. It is lawful for any number of persons to meet together for the *sole* purpose of *consulting* and determining upon the rate of wages which *the persons present at such meeting, or any of them*, shall require or demand for his or their work.

2nd. Or, to meet together for the sole purpose of *consulting* and determining upon the rate of prices which the persons present at such meeting or any of them shall require or demand, for his or their work.

3rd. Or, to meet together for the sole purpose of

consulting upon and determining the rate of wages or prices which the persons present at such meeting, or any of them, shall require or demand for the hours or time for which he or they shall work in any manufacture, trade, or business.

With respect to agreements of workmen and others: *Agreements of workmen.*

1st. It is lawful for any number of persons to enter into *any agreement*, verbal or written, amongst themselves, for the purpose of fixing the rate of *wages* which the parties entering into such agreement, or any of them, shall require or demand for his or their work.

2nd. Or, for the purpose of fixing the rate of *prices* which the parties entering into such agreement, or any of them, shall require or demand for his or their work.

3rd. Or, for the purpose of fixing the rate of wages or prices, which the parties entering into such agreement, or any of them, shall require or demand for the hours or time for which he or they will work in any manufacture, trade or business.

With respect to the meetings and agreements of *Meetings of Masters.* masters, it is enacted, by the 5th section, that persons present at the following meetings, or entering into the following agreements, shall be exempted from any punishment, penalty or prosecution.

1st. It is lawful for any number of persons to meet together for the *sole purpose* of consulting upon and determining *the rate of wages* which the persons present at such meeting, or any of them, shall pay his or their journeymen, workmen, or servants, for their work.

2nd. Or for the sole purpose of consulting upon and determining the *rate of prices*, which the persons present at such meeting, or any of them, shall pay to his or their journeymen, workmen, or servants, for their work.

3rd. Or for the sole purpose of consulting upon and determining the rate of wages or prices which the persons present at such meeting, or any of them, shall pay to his or their journeymen, workmen, or servants for *the hours or time of working* in any manufacture, trade, or business.

Agreement of masters.

And with respect to agreements, it is lawful for any number of persons to enter into any agreement, verbal or written, among themselves.

1st. For the purpose of fixing the rate of *wages* which the parties entering into such agreement, or any of them, shall pay to his or their journeymen, workmen, or servants for their work.

2nd. Or for the purpose of fixing the rate of *prices* which the parties entering into such agreement, or any of them, shall pay to his or their journeymen, workmen, or servants for their work.

3rd. Or for the purpose of fixing the rate of wages or prices which the parties entering into such agreement, or any of them, shall pay to his or their journeymen, workmen, or servants, for *the hours or time of working* in any manufacture, trade, or business.

Combinations —lawful, under what restrictions.

It will be perceived, from the above specification, that the act of 6th Geo. 4th legalises some combinations, both of masters and workmen, under certain restrictions.—1st. The meeting or combination must appear to have been formed for the sole purpose of fixing the rate of wages or prices, or determining upon the rate of wages or prices to be paid according to the hours or time of working.—2nd. It must also appear that no determination, or resolution, or agreement of any kind was entered into, purporting to affect any person not present at the meeting; the parties present at such a meeting may enter into a written agreement among themselves—a particular portion of a trade may meet together to regulate the prices to be paid for their own labour ; but should any determination be made, or resolution formed, for the purpose of fixing or arranging the wages of the entire trade, such a meeting is not protected within the provisions of the 4th and 5th sections of the statute. However, should any persons meet for a purpose not contemplated by the statute, as for example, to limit the number of apprentices in any particular trade, and, to effect this object, enter into an agreement intended merely to bind themselves,—yet,—as such a meeting is not included in the statute, the persons present would not be protected by its provisions. Previous to the 6th Geo. IV. it was illegal, by the common law, for persons to meet or combine for the purpose of raising or lessening the wages of labor,—[r] but now such a meeting or combination may be lawful if restricted within its proper limits; and it is advisable that an agreement in writing should be always entered into, clearly defining the object of the combined body, and that it was not intended, in any manner, to influence or affect any person not present at the meeting, or not a party to the agreement; this precaution is necessary, in order that the object of such an association may be known, and its members protected from prosecution.

Agreement ought to be in writing.

[r] See ante page 4.

Certain offences prohibited by the statute, not prohibited at common law.

Certain combinations permitted by the statute, prohibited by the common law.

Unlawful societies.

Having now classified and detailed both the offences prohibited as well as the privileges permitted by the 6th of Geo. IV., it may be added that many of the offences created by the third section of that statute were unknown at the common law. Thus, the mere molestation or obstruction of another in his trade or occupation, if unaccompanied by violence, would not be considered the subject of an indictment without a previous combination or confederacy; and, on the other side, certain combinations or agreements prohibited by the common law, are permitted by the statute,—its 4th and 5th sections render certain associations legal which otherwise would be indictable; but with the exception of such meetings or combinations as are expressly within the provisions of those sections, the common law, as it affects the confederacies both of employers and employed, is now in full force and operation. It is a mistake, therefore, to suppose that the 6th of Geo. IV. repealed the combination laws. It merely repealed the statutory enactments,—leaving to the common law, with the sole exception above stated, its full force and power of opposing and repressing, in the manner endeavoured to be explained in the preceding chapter,— every species of confederacy injurious to an individual or in restraint of public trade. But, in addition to the common law, there are two statutes, the 50 Geo. III. c. 102, and the 4th of Geo. IV. c. 87, enacted (among other purposes) to suppress certain unlawful societies, and certain associations bound by an oath or engagement,—the nature of which shall be fully explained in the next chapter, so far as they affect the combinations of master and workman.

With respect to assaults arising out of unlawful combination,—there is a section in the 10th Geo. IV. c. 34, (the act for consolidating and amending the statutes in Ireland relating to offences against the person) which, —as it has been especially enacted for the punishment of persons committing such offences—shall be briefly explained. By the 28*th section* it is enacted, " that if " any person shall, in consequence of any unlawful " combination or conspiracy respecting any trade, " business, or manufacture, or respecting any person " concerned or employed therein,—unlawfully and ma- " liciously assault any person with intent to do such " person any grievous bodily harm—every such offender " shall be liable to be transported beyond the seas for " the term of seven years,—or to be imprisoned, with " or without hard labour, in the common gaol or house " of correction, for any term not exceeding three years, " and if a male, to be once, twice, or thrice privately " whipped (if the court shall think fit) in addition to " such imprisonment."

Assaults arising out of illegal combination. Evidence, necessary to convict.

An assault is, any attempt to offer with force or violence to do a corporal injury to another; and upon an indictment under this section of the statute, it is not necessary to prove that any grievous bodily harm was inflicted upon the person assaulted. All that is necessary to prove is the intent required by the statute, and that the assault was committed in consequence of an unlawful combination. In order to prove the intent, it is necessary to know the meaning of the words "grievous bodily harm;" some of the judges have held, that to constitute grievous bodily harm, it should appear that the injury intended to be inflicted would be permanent; however, Bushe, Chief Justice,[t] thought that a wound which would disable the prosecutor from working for a week was such an injury, as to make a case sufficient to be sent to a jury; so that upon an indictment under this section of the statute, if it should appear that an assault was committed, with the intention of inflicting such an injury as would endanger the life of the person assaulted,—or would prevent him from pursuing his ordinary occupation for some time; it seems that this would be sufficient to go to a jury, as evidence of the offence.

Felonies connected with combination.

There was another crime, supposed to be connected with illegal combination, which was punished with the utmost severity by the 10th Geo. IV. c. 34.,[u] namely, —the offence of maliciously throwing or applying to any person, any corrosive or noxious liquid or substance, with the intention of maiming, disfiguring, or disabling such person, or of doing him some other grievous bodily harm. This was a capital felony, by the 15th section of that act, if death ensuing therefrom, would amount to murder; but a late statute, the 1st of Queen Victoria, c. 85, repeals this part of the statute

Injuries to the person.

and enacts that, "whosoever shall unlawfully and " maliciously send or deliver, or cause to be taken or "received by any person, any explosive substance, or " any other dangerous thing, or shall cast or throw "upon, or otherwise apply to any person any corro- " sive fluid or other destructive matter, with intent in " any of the cases aforesaid, to burn, maim, disfigure, " or disable any person, or to do some other grievous " bodily harm to any person—or whereby in any of the

[t] *Rex* v. *Philips and others,* and see *Rex* v. *Lavery and another,* 4 *L. R. (N. S.)* 153.

[u] Analogous to 9th Geo. IV. ch. 31, Eng.

" cases aforesaid, any person shall be burnt, maimed,
" disfigured or disabled, or shall receive some other
" grievous bodily harm, such person shall be guilty of
" *felony*, and being convicted thereof, shall be liable,
" at the discretion of the Court, to be *transported for*
" *life, or for not less than fifteen years, or to be impri-*
" *soned for not less than three years.* And the offender
" may, if imprisoned, be kept to hard labour—or in so-
" litary confinement, not exceeding one month at a
" time." [v]

The first portion of the above section appears to
be principally directed against offenders sending or
delivering, or causing to be received in letters, pack-
ages, or otherwise, explosive substances, calculated to
burn or severely injure the person. As to the second
part of the section, it embraces the crime of vitriol-
throwing, which of late years has become not an unusual offence. If a person be charged with the intent
of committing any of the offences mentioned in this section, the intent ought to be proved, as laid,—although
the purpose intended was not in fact effected : and
the prisoner's motives and intentions may be inferred
from the means which he uses and the acts which he
does. [w] It should also appear that the explosive substance, corrosive fluid, or other destructive matter
was of the nature intended by the statute.

With respect to the malicious destruction of machi- Injuries to
property.
nery, and goods in a state of manufacture, it is
enacted by the 9th Geo. IV. c. 56, [x]

" Sect. 3. That if any person shall unlawfully and

[v] See 5th section of 1st Victoria, c. 85.
[w] 2 *Starkie Evid.* 500, 2d *Edit.*
[x] Analogous to 7th and 8th Geo. IV. c. 30, Eng.

" maliciously cut, break, or destroy, or damage, with
" intent to destroy or render useless, any goods or arti-
" cles of silk, woollen, mohair or cotton, or of any one
" of those materials mixed with each other, or mixed
" with any other materials, or any framework, knitted
" piece, stocking hose, or lace in the loom or frame, or
" on any machine or engine, or on the rack or tenters,
" or in any stage, process, or progress of manufacture;
" or shall unlawfully and maliciously cut, break, or
" destroy, or damage, with intent to destroy or to
" render useless any warp or shute of silk, linen,
" woollen, muslin, cotton, or of any one or more of
" those materials mixed with each other or mixed with
" any other material, or any loom, frame, machine,
" engine, rack, tackle, tool, or implement, whether
" fixed or moveable, prepared for or employed in manu-
" facturing or preparing any such goods or articles ; or
" shall by force enter into any house, shop, building,
" or place, with intent to commit any of the offences
" aforesaid, every such offender shall be guilty of fel-
" ony, and being convicted thereof, shall be liable, at
" the discretion of the Court, *to be transported for*
" *life, or not less than seven years, or to be imprisoned*
" *for not exceeding four, and if a male, to be whipped,*
" *(if the Court shall think fit,) in addition to impri-*
" *sonment.*" And the 4th section (amongst other
things enacts,) that if any person shall unlawfully and
" maliciously cut, break, or destroy or damage, with
" intent to destroy or to render useless, any machine
" or engine, whether fixed or moveable, prepared for
" or employed in any manufacture whatsoever, (except
" the machinery used in the manufacture of the arti-
" cles in 3rd section,) every such person shall be

39

"guilty of felony. The punishment is *transportation*
"*for seven years, or imprisonment for not exceeding two,*
"*and if a mae, whipping,* (if the Court shall so think
"fit,) *in addition to such imprisonment.*"

Those sections enumerate a variety of separate
offences, and the proofs generally will be : 1st,
proof of the unlawful and malicious act; 2d, the
nature of the property injured, which must appear to
be within the statute ; 3d, the property of the prosecutor; 4th, the intent and malice. As to what is a
destruction of a machine; it has been held in several
cases that it is an offence within the statute, though
previous to the time when the machine was broken, it
had been taken to pieces, and was in different places,
only requiring a carpenter to put those pieces together ; *Mackerel's case*, 4 *C. & P.* 448.[y] And as to
forcibly entering into a house, the intent must be
proved as laid ; thus where prisoners were charged
with breaking into a house, with intent to cut and
destroy certain tools employed in making woollen
goods, and it appeared that the article destroyed was
part of the loom itself, they were held to be properly
acquitted,—the intent not being proved.[z]

And by the 5th section of the same statute, "if
"any artificer, workman, journeyman, apprentice,
"servant or labourer, should wilfully and unlawfully
"damage, spoil, or destroy goods, wares, or work,
"committed to his care or charge, without the con-
"sent of his employer, upon conviction before a jus-
"tice of the peace, he forfeits a sum not exceeding

Of the evi- dence.

Wilful injuries by workmen to property com- mitted to their charge.

[y] *And see Fidler's case* 4, *C. & P.* 449. *Chubb's case*, 2 *Deac. Dig. C. L.* 151.
[z] *Hill's case, Russ and Ry.* 483.

" £5 to the party grieved, or in default of payment, " he may be imprisoned, with or without hard labour, " for any period not exceeding three months."

This last section is confined to the mere wilful and unlawful damage or destruction of goods or work committed to the charge of workmen, &c. and the wilful intention may generally be presumed from the unlawful act, unaccompanied by any circumstances justifying its commission.

Although it is not the object of this Treatise to digest the criminal law relating to offences that might arise from illegal combination ; yet—as the above sections of the statutes were principally enacted for the purpose of suppressing and prohibiting crimes that frequently follow such combinations—it was thought proper that those sections should be extracted and briefly explained.

The administration of unlawful oaths or engagements,—and the nature of secret societies or unlawful combinations, bound by any oath or engagement, shall now be explained, so far as they affect the relations of master and workman.

CHAPTER III.

OF UNLAWFUL OATHS, OF SECRET SOCIETIES, AND
OTHER UNLAWFUL COMBINATIONS.

IT has already been observed that the Common Law
has always been repugnant to every kind of confederacy, interfering with, or impeding the free use and
enjoyment of labor and capital. Several statutes,—
some of which have been enumerated in the preceding
chapter—were passed for the purpose of extending the
power and increasing the rigor of the Common Law.
The Legislature deemed it both wise and salutary, by
the 6th Geo. IV. c. 129, to repeal those statutes and all
other enactments relative to combinations, formed for
the purpose of arranging the rate of wages, the time of
working, the quantity of work, or mode of conducting any manufacture : but it was by no means
intended, nor did the latter statute, in fact, affect
certain unlawful associations, peculiar in their nature,
the members of which are in general united by some
unlawful oath, or declaration, or engagement. The
statutes passed for the purpose of prohibiting the administration or taking of such unlawful oaths, and for
the suppression of such associations, although not
confined to the combinations of master and workman,

yet may embrace such combinations within their provisions. The parts or sections of those statutes relating to such unlawful oaths and confederacies shall therefore be explained, with the nature of the offences arising therefrom.

Of the administration of unlawful Oaths.

The offence of taking or administering unlawful oaths is provided for by the 50th Geo, III. c. 52,[a] passed on the 20th of June, 1810.

From its preamble, which recites that wicked and evil disposed persons had attempted to seduce several of His Majesty's subjects in Ireland from their allegiance, and to associate them under the pretended obligations of oaths unlawfully administered; it might be supposed that the statute was directed against combinations for the purpose of mutiny and sedition; but the enacting part is much more extensive in its terms, and embraces other more general objects. It will appear from a few cases cited hereafter,[b] that it includes the taking or administering of unlawful oaths by members of illegal societies of tradesmen and others,—and that portion of the act which expressly affects the members of such combinations, shall now be detailed and explained. It enacts, in its first section, that the following persons shall be guilty of administering an unlawful oath or engagement.[c] 1st.

What persons shall be guilty of the administration of such Oaths.

Any person or persons who shall administer or cause to be administered. 2nd. any person or persons who shall tender or cause to be tendered. 3rd. Any person or persons who shall be present, aiding and assisting, at the administering or tendering to any

---

[a] Analogous to the 37th Geo. 3. c. 123, Eng.

[b] See post, pages 46, 47.   [c] See 1st Section.

person or persons in Ireland, upon a book or otherwise. 4th. Any person or persons who shall, by threats, promises, persuasions, or under undue means, cause, procure, or induce to be taken by any person or persons in Ireland upon a book or otherwise, any or either of the following oaths or engagements. 1st. Any oath or engagement importing to bind the person What oaths or persons taking the same to be of any association, unlawful. brotherhood, committee, society, or confederacy whatsoever, under whatever name, description, or pretence—such association, brotherhood, committee, society, or confederacy, shall assume, or pretend to be formed or constituted,—if in reality *formed* (amongst other objects) to injure the persons or property of any person or persons whatsoever. 2nd. Or *to be formed* to injure the persons or property of any persons whatsoever. 3rd. Or formed to compel any person or persons whatsoever *to do any act* or acts whatsoever. 4th. Or *to be formed* to compel any person or persons whatsoever *to do any act* or acts whatsoever. 5th. Or formed to compel any person or persons whatsoever to *omit or refuse* to do any act or acts whatsoever. 6th. Or *to be formed,* &c. (for the above purpose.) 7th. Or any oath or engagement importing to bind the person taking the same *to obey* the orders, or rules, or commands of any *committee* or other body of men not lawfully constituted. 8th. Or to *assemble* at the desire and command of any *such committee,* or of any person or persons not having lawful authority. 9th. Or any oath or engagement importing to bind the person taking the same *not to inform or give evidence* against any brother, associate, confederate, or other person. 10th. Or not *to reveal or discover any* illegal act done

44

or to be done. 11th. Or not *to discover* any illegal oath or engagement, or the import of any such illegal oath or engagement which may be administered or tendered to him or her, whether such oath shall be afterwards so administered or tendered or not,—or whether he or she shall take such oath, or enter into

Punishment. such engagement or not;—every person convicted of any or either of the offences above enumerated, shall be adjudged guilty of *felony, and transported for life;*

Who are principal offenders. and not only the persons above enumerated, but by the 3rd section[d] it is expressly enacted, "that all " persons present, aiding and assisting at the adminis- " tering or tendering of any such oath or engagement, " and all persons causing any such oath or engagement " to be administered or tendered,—though not present, " shall be deemed *principal offenders* and tried as " such, though the person or persons who actually " administered or tendered such oath or engagement " shall not have been tried or convicted."

Punishment of persons taking the unlawful oath or engagement. And with respect to the punishment of a person *taking* such an oath or engagement, it is by the 1st section provided, that every person who shall *take,* in Ireland, any such oath or engagement importing so to bind him or her, as in the said section stated, being convicted thereof, shall be adjudged guilty of *felony, and be transported for seven years.*[e]

Disclosure of facts by prisoner—evidence for him. But by the 2nd section it is provided "that any " person or persons who may have been compelled

<hr>

[d] See the 3rd section.

[e] So by section 6 of 27 Geo. 3, c. 15 (Irish) the administering an unlawful oath is a felony, punished by transportation for life,—the taking of such an oath a felony, punished by transportation for seven years.

[f] See 2nd section.

45

" by inevitable necessity to commit any of the offences
" aforesaid, upon proof of such inevitable necessity,
" shall be excused and justified, provided that no
" such inevitable necessity shall justify or excuse any
" such person or persons, unless he, she, or they shall
" within ten days, if not prevented by actual force or
" sickness, and then within seven days after such
" actual force or sickness shall cease to disable
" him, her, or them, from giving information of the
" same, disclose to a justice of the peace in the county
" in which he, she, or they shall then be, by infor-
" mation on oath, the whole of what he, she, or they
" know touching the compelling him, her, or them
" to commit any such offence, and of the person or
" persons by whom he, she, or they were compelled
" to commit such offence, and who were present at
" the time such offence was committed, and of the
" place where the same was committed: Provided,
" however, that no person shall be so excluded from the
" defence of inevitable necessity, who shall be tried
" for the said offence, within the said period of ten
" days from the commission of such offence, or of seven
" days from the time when such force or sickness
" shall cease as aforesaid." In order to escape the penalty of the statute, it is not sufficient for the prisoner
merely to prove that he took the oath or engagement
under compulsion. It must appear that he complied
with the requisition of the statute,—that within ten
days,—unless labouring under the disability of actual
force or sickness, or within seven days after the cessation of such disability,—he disclosed to a magistrate,
by information upon oath, the whole of the compulsion known to him,—by whom compelled,—the persons

46

present at the commission of the offence,—and the place where the same was committed.

What oaths within the statute.

This statute is not confined to oaths administered for seditious or mutinous purposes, for it has been decided the unlawful administering, by any associated body of men, of an oath to any person, purporting to bind him not to reveal or discover such unlawful combination or conspiracy, nor any illegal act done by them,—was within the analogous statute[g] in England. As in the case of the *King* v. *Marks*[h] *and others*, where it appeared that certain journeymen shearmen, in consequence of a dispute with the master clothiers about the rate of wages, appointed a committee from themselves to regulate their trade, and that the committee required every journeyman shearman to take a certain oath to the effect that, " he would be true to every " journeyman shearman, and not to hurt any of them, " and that he would not divulge any of their secrets ;" that upon taking the oath he received a ticket which entitled him to get work, and, that in order to compel every journeyman shearman to belong to this association, the members of it objected to work with those who had not such tickets. Although the object of this association was merely to raise wages and regulate a certain trade, yet, it was held that the administration of such an oath was a *felony;* so also in the case of the *King* v. *Ball and others*,[1] where an oath was administered, that the party taking it should keep all secrets of the lodge, and should not make an article of trade (buttons) under certain prices ; it was decided to be an administering of an oath within the statute.

[g] The 37th Geo. 3. c. 123.   [h] 3 *East.* 157.   [i] 6 *Car. & Pay.* 563.

So the administering an oath or engagement to any person not to reveal the secrets of any association is an offence within the statute;[k] in this case it appeared, from the deposition of one Eliza Beswick, that she, with several other persons, (buttonmakers,) assembled, at a public house where a trade's union was held, that one Brunt (a deputy) came to them and told them it would be for their good to enter a union— that their eyes being bound with handkerchiefs, with their left hands on the Bible, they solemnly declared they would not make buttons under certain prices, and that they would keep all secrets of the lodge. It appeared that the prisoners were all present at the initiation—they pleaded guilty, and were recommended to mercy. Mr. Justice Williams said, that " no man, " who has the fairness or industry to peruse the acts " of parliament, and understand them, can entertain " a doubt that to administer an oath or engagement " not to reveal the secrets of the association is within " the statute ;" the same point was also decided in the case of the *King* v. *Brodripp*.[1]

With respect to the nature of the oath, it is immaterial what its form may be, if it was intended to make the parties to whom it was administered believe themselves under an engagement ; and it is an oath within the statute if it was understood by the party tendering it and by the party taking it, as having the force and obligation of an oath; and it is not material whether the book upon which the oath was administered was a testament or not, provided the party taking the oath believes himself to be under a binding

[k] *Ibid.*   *Ibid.* 571.

48

obligation. [m] Should the terms of the oath be ambiguous, the declarations of the party administering it, made at the time, will be admitted in evidence, in order to show the meaning of those terms; [n] so also the party who complies with the terms of an illegal oath, is a competent witness on an indictment for administering it; and it is not necessary that the party should either repeat the oath or kiss the book. [o] In this case, which was an indictment under the 27th Geo. 3rd, c. 15, sect. 6, (the Riot Act,) which makes it a felony to administer "any unlawful oath or solemn "engagement," it appeared that the oath was pronounced by the prisoner, but was not repeated after him by the witness, neither did the witness kiss the book—it was objected that his omission to repeat the oath or to kiss the book, was fatal; but Jebb J. overruled the objection.

Secret societies and illegal combinations bound by an oath or engagement.

There is another statute enacted for the purpose of amending and rendering more effectual the provisions of the 50th Geo. 3rd, c. 102, and for the suppression of certain illegal combinations, to which attention is particularly desired. It is the 4th of Geo. 4th, c. 87, and was passed on the 18th July, 1823. This act includes within its provisions many illegal combinations and societies, and prosecutions have been frequently instituted upon the corresponding statutes in England [p] against workmen, as members of such com-

[m] *Rex* v. *Brodripp*, 6 *Carr, & Pay.* 571; *Rex* v. *Lovelass and others*, 1 *Moo. & Rob.* 349.

[n] *Moor's case*, 6 *East*, 419.

[o] *Rex* v. *Hayes*, *Clare Spe. Com. June*, 1831, *Hayes' Crim. Law*, 150. And as to the construction of this statute, see *Rex.* v. *Adams*, *Maryborough Spe. Com. June*, 1832.

[p] The 39th Geo. III. c. 79, sect. 2, and 57th Geo. III. c. 19, sect 25.

binations : an attempt will, therefore, now be made clearly to specify the offences it prohibits, so far as they relate to master aad workman, and a few examples will then be given, of what have been decided to be illegal combinations and confederacies within the corresponding statute. The several offences prohibited by this statute shall in the first instance be detailed —the persons deemed offenders shall then be stated.

The first section, [q] after reciting that it was expedient that so much of the 50th Geo. 3rd, c. 102, as relates to unlawful oaths should be rendered more effectual—enacts, that after the expiration of fourteen days after the passing of the act, every society, association, brotherhood, committee, lodge, club, or confederacy whatsoever, then established or thereafter to be established in Ireland,—of the nature thereinafter described, shall be deemed and taken to be an unlawful combination and confederacy. *The offences prohibited by the statute.*

The following are the unlawful combinations and confederacies :

1st. Every society, association, brotherhood, committee, lodge, club, or confederacy, the members whereof shall, according to the rules thereof,—or according to any provision or agreement for that purpose, —be required or admitted or permitted to take any oath or engagement which shall be an unlawful oath or engagement, within the intent and meaning of the said 50th Geo. 3rd, c. 102. *Unlawful combinations and confederacies*

2nd. Or shall be required or admitted or permitted to take any oath not required or authorised by law.

3rd. And any and every society, association, brotherhood,—committee, lodge, club or confederacy, the members whereof or any of them, shall take, or in any manner bind themselves by any such oath or engagement, upon becoming, or in consequence of being members of such society, &c.

4th. Or the members whereof shall take, subscribe, or assent to any test or declaration not required by law.

5th. Or of which the names of the members or any of them shall be kept secret from the society at large.

6th. Or which shall have any committee or select body chosen or appointed in such a manner, that the members constituting the same may not be known by the society at large to be members of such committee or select body.

7th. Or which shall have any president, treasurer, secretary, delegate, or other officer chosen or appointed in such a manner that the election or appointment of such persons to such offices may not be known to the society at large.

8th. Or of which the names of all the members and of all committees or select bodies of members, and of all presidents, treasurers, secretaries, delegates or other officers shall not be entered in a book or books to be kept for that purpose, and to be open to the inspection of all the members of such society.

The following persons shall by this statute be deemed guilty of an unlawful combination and confederacy :

Persons guilty of an unlawful combination and confederacy.

1st. Every person, who, at any time after the expiration of fourteen days next after the passing of the act, should become a member of any such society, association, brotherhood, committee, lodge, club, or confederacy.

2nd. Or who, being a member of any such society, &c. at the time of the passing of the act, should afterwards act as a member thereof.

3rd. Every person, who, after the expiration of fourteen days next after the passing of this act, shall directly or indirectly, maintain correspondence or intercourse with any such society, &c.—or with any division, branch, lodge, committee, or other select body, president, treasurer, secretary, delegate, or other officer or member thereof as such.

4th. Or who shall, by contribution of money or otherwise, aid, abet, or support any such society, &c. or any member or officer thereof as such. So also a person once convicted—for knowingly permitting any meeting of any society—by the act declared to be an unlawful combination or confederacy—or of any division, branch, or committee of such society—to be held in his or her house or apartment, shall for a subsequent offence be deemed guilty of an unlawful combination and confederacy.[r]

By the second section, it is provided that the provisions of this statute shall not extend to any declaration to be taken, subscribed, or assented to by the members of any society—in case the form of such declaration shall have been first approved and subscribed by the magistrates of the county, city, town or place where such society shall ordinarily assemble, —and shall have been registered with the clerk of the peace or his deputy, for such county, city, town, or

Not to extend to the declaration of members of any society, if approved of by Justices.

---

[r] See the 7th section of the act, post page 56.

place ; but the approbation of the magistrates shall only remain valid and effectual, until the next general sessions for such county, &c. unless the same shall be confirmed by the major part of the justices present at such general sessions.

Mode of trial and punishment.

The mode of trial directed by this statute is either a summary proceeding before two justices of the peace for the county, city, or town where the person accused should happen to be; or by indictment, to be preferred in the county or city where the offence was alleged to be committed. Should the former mode of proceeding be adopted, the justices have power to hear and determine the case and punish the offender by an imprisonment of three calendar months, or by a fine of twenty pounds;—with a power of reducing one third of such punishment of fine or imprisonment, (should they so think fit). If an offender should be convicted upon an indictment, he may be *transported for seven years*, or he may be sentenced to an imprisonment with hard labour,—or he may be imprisoned for any time not exceeding two years, as the court before whom the offence has been tried, should think fit.

A principal difference between the 50th Geo. 3rd, c. 102, and the 4th Geo. 4th, c. 87, [s] is, that by the former statute, the administering or taking an oath or engagement for any of the purposes therein mentioned is a felony—whereas by the latter statute, any association united by a similar oath or engagement, is declared to be an illegal combination and confederacy ;

[s] The 6th Geo. 4th, c. 4, sect 3, extended the 4th Geo. 4th, c. 87, to societies therein named, but it (the 6th Geo. 4th,) has since expired.

53

and the persons connected with, or having intercourse or correspondence with its members *as such*, made liable to punishment.

The evidence necessary to establish a conviction under the 4th Geo. 4th, c. 87, will be—1st, proof of the existence of such a society as is prohibited by the statute; 2nd, proof of the prisoner's connection, intercourse, or correspondence with such a society, or his aid or support of it. With respect to the evidence of the existence of the society, and the prisoner's connection with it, many of the observations in the first chapter, relative to the proof of combination at Common Law, will apply with equal force to proceedings under the statute. Several prosecutions by indictment have lately been instituted in England under the corresponding statutes, and artizans and others convicted for a violation of their provisions.

Thus in the case of the *King* v. *Lovelass and others*,[t] it was decided that an association, the members of which are bound by an oath not to disclose its secrets, is an unlawful combination and conspiracy, (unless expressly declared by some act of Parliament to be

Of the evidence.

An association, for whatever purpose formed, the members of which are bound by an

[t] 1 *Moo. & Rob.* 349; 6 *Carr & Pay.* 597. This case (the Dorchester labourers) is remarkable for the interest which it excited amongst the working classes in all parts of the country. Numerous petitions were presented to both Houses of Parliament, praying a remission of the sentence, and the subject underwent considerable discussion: on the 21st of April, 1834, the Trades' Union of the metropolis marched in procession to the number of from 25,000 to 30,000 men from Copenhagen Fields to Whitehall, through the streets of London, with a petition to his late Majesty, said to have been signed by 266,000 persons. The then Secretary of State (Lord Melbourne) having declined to receive a petition so presented,—it was afterwards presented by a deputation. The sentence of transportation has subsequently been remitted.

oath not to dis-
close its secrets
is an unlawful
combination
and confede-
racy.

legal,) for whatever purpose or object it may be formed; and the administering an oath not to reveal any thing done in the association is an offence within the statute. In this case the prisoners were labourers. It appeared that the oath was administered by one of the prisoners, in the presence of the others, to the witness, who was blindfolded, and that something was said about keeping secret what was done in the society; and that in a box belonging to one of the prisoners was found a book, headed " General Rules." The substance of the rules was, that there should be a lodge in every parish, a committee and contributions to support those who were willing to quit their work when desired; that no person should turn out for advance of wages without consent of the Grand Lodge; that no member should work with any man who acted contrary to the rules prescribed by the Grand Lodge; that no person should be admitted to the meetings when drunk, and that they should not countenance any violence or violation of the laws of the realm. The prisoners were found guilty and transported. *See note (t.)*

Every member
of an associa-
tion, who in
consequence of
being so, takes
any oath not
required by law
is guilty of an
illegal combi-
nation and con-
federacy.

In the case of the *King* v. *Dixon*[u] it was also decided, that every person who engaged in an association, the members of which, in consequence of being so, take any oath not required by law, is guilty of an offence within the statute, 57th Geo. 3rd, c. 19[v] In this case it appeared, that in March, 1834, there existed in Cambridge a trades' union of the operative cordwainers of that town; the object of which was to

[u] 6 *Carr. & Pay.* 602.
[v] Corresponding with 4th Geo. 4th, c. 87.

make a powerful confederacy to protect labour ; the members were bound by an oath not to reveal the secrets of the association. Bosanquet, Justice, said, " I " have no hesitation whatever in saying, that confe- " deracies like that which appears to have existed in " the present case, are as decidedly in contravention " of the law of the land, as they are pregnant with " mischief to the community, and to the working " classes themselves. It is for the sake of those who " belong to associations like the late Cordwainer's " Union of Cambridge, that I now declare that all " who engage in associations, the members of which, " in consequence of being so, take any oaths not re- " quired by law, are guilty of an offence against the " statute, which, if clearly proved, would, upon " conviction, be in every case, followed by ex- " emplary punishment. It is impossible that any " well ordered state of society could tolerate the " existence of confederacies bound together by se- " cret compacts and oaths not required by law,—one " of the obvious consequences of such confederacies " being, to deprive the state of the benefit of the tes- " timony of those who are engaged in them,—a state " of things injurious to the individuals, subversive of " public order, and striking at the very existence of " the state, by withdrawing the allegiance of the sub- " ject from the laws of the land to the secret tribu- " nals of unlawful societies,—constraining the con- " science by oaths, and seeking to obtain their objects, " whatever they might be, by popular intimidation." ʷ

ʷ A good deal of discussion has lately taken place in Parliament upon the presentation of a petition by Mr. Wakley, respecting the Glasgow cotton spinners. It was strenuously contended by that honor-

56

56

Penalty on persons permitting unlawful societies to meet in their houses.

Not only is a severe punishment attached to the offence of unlawful combination and confederacy by this statute, (4 Geo. 4th, c. 87,) but a heavy penalty is inflicted on persons permitting unlawful meetings in their houses ;—for by the 7th section of this act it is provided, that if any person knowingly permit any meeting of any society, declared to be an unlawful combination and confederacy, or of any division, branch, or committee of such society, to be held in his or her house or apartment, such person shall, for the first offence, forfeit the sum of five pounds ; and for a subsequent offence shall be *deemed guilty of an unlawful combination and confederacy* against that statute.

Not necessary to be a member of an unlawful society to incur the guilt of unlawful combination and confederacy, nor is it necessary that its object should be unlawful.

It only remains again to repeat that to establish conviction under this statute, it is not necessary that the person convicted should be actually a member of an unlawful combination, any person who directly or indirectly maintains correspondence or intercourse with the unlawful society, or with any officer or member of it in his official capacity, or contributes by money or otherwise to the aid or support of such a society, or to the aid or support of any officer or member of it as such, is equally guilty, and if con-

able member, that the sentence pronounced against them was illegal, and that if convicted in England, the punishment could only be three months' imprisonment. It would be most presumptuous in the writer to attempt to give any opinion respecting the law of Scotland ; but he conceives that if the prisoners were indicted in England, as members of a secret or unlawful association, united by an oath or engagement—the evidence of the witnesses Moat, Murdock, Cowan, and others, might be sufficient to go to a jury, as proof of their guilt. And if, upon such evidence, they were convicted, the sentence would be precisely the same as that pronounced in the High Court of Justiciary—namely, transportation for seven years.

victed upon an indictment, may be *transported for seven years.* Nor is it necessary that the object of the society should be unlawful,—its object may be perfectly legitimate,—as for example, to regulate the wages of its members,—but should the persons assembled in such society unite themselves by an oath or engagement, it then becomes unlawful, and its members guilty of an unlawful combination.

The writer having now endeavoured to digest and explain the common and statute law, relating to the combinations of persons engaged in trade or manufactures, may venture briefly to analyse the rights and liabilities both of the employer and the employed. Every man has a right to dispose of his own labor, capital, and skill in the mode he may deem most conducive to his own advantage.

Any number of men may unite for the purpose of affixing a price, or estimating the value of their own combined labor, or capital, or skill.

But no man has a right to impede or obstruct another in the disposal of his own labor, capital, or skill,—or to dictate to him the price or the value to be affixed to such labor or capital; and no body of men have a right to unite and combine for the purpose of impeding, obstructing, or in any manner restraining another, in the disposition or the management of his own labour or capital.

And no man nor any body of men, even for a legitimate object, can become connected, or have intercourse with any secret or otherwise unlawful association.

Conclusion. Although the offence of combination, and the crimes arising therefrom, have been the principal object of this little treatise; and it was not the intention of the writer to take notice of the disputes and disagreements which frequently occur between master and workman, arising out of breaches of civil contract or agreement, yet, he cannot avoid briefly referring to a very useful and important statute, enacted for the purpose of settling such disagreements in a satisfactory and expeditious manner.—It is the 5th Geo. 4th, c. 96. It directs that disagreements respecting payment, or about the hours of working, compensation to workmen for purchase or alteration of implements to work new pattern; disputes respecting the length, breadth, or quality of pieces of goods; disputes in the cotton manufacture; disputes respecting wages or compensation for pieces of goods that are made of any great or extraordinary length,—or arising out of the particular trade, or manufacture, or contracts relative thereto, which cannot be otherwise adjusted, may be settled by reference to a justice of the peace by mutual consent; or on complaint of either party, he may appoint four or six arbitrators, half masters, half workmen of the place, of the former of whom the master, of the latter the workman may choose one, to finally determine. The arbitrators have power to investigate the complaint,—to examine witnesses, and to make an award which shall be final and conclusive, in case the award be made within three days after the appointment of them as referees; otherwise the justice of the peace who appointed them, or any other justice in his absence, may finally determine. A manufacturer or his agent cannot act as a justice.

This is a most useful statute, and perhaps if generally known, may sometimes prevent many of the offences which it has been the object of this work to digest and explain.

ANNO SEXTO

GEORGII IV. REGIS.

CHAP. CXXIX.

An Act to repeal the Laws relating to the Combination of Workmen, and to make other Provisions in lieu thereof.

[6th *July*, 1825.]

WHEREAS an Act was passed in the last session of Parliament, intituled an Act to repeal the laws relative to the combination of workmen, and for other purposes therein mentioned, by which Act various statutes and parts of statutes relating to combinations among workmen for fixing the wages of labour, and for regulating or controlling the mode of carrying on any manufacture, trade, or business, were repealed, and other provisions were made for protecting the free employment of capital and labour, and for punishing combinations interfering with such freedom, by means of violence, threats, or intimidation : and whereas the provisions of the said Act have not been found effectual: and whereas such combinations are injurious to trade and commerce, dangerous to the tranquillity of the country, and especially prejudicial to the interests of all who are concerned in them : and whereas it is expedient to make further provision, as well for the security and personal freedom of individual workmen in the disposal of their skill and labour, as for the security of the property and persons of masters and employers, and for that purpose to repeal the said Act, and to enact other provisions and regulations in lieu thereof : be it therefore enacted by the king's most

(margin note: 5 G. 4. c. 95.)

excellent majesty, by and with the advice and consent of the lords spiritual and temporal, and commons, in this present parliament assembled, and by the authority of the same, that from and after the passing of this Act the said recited Act of the last session of parliament shall be and the same is hereby repealed.

Recited Act repealed.

II. Provided always, and be it enacted, that from and after the passing of this Act, so much of an Act made in the thirty-third year of the reign of king Edward the first, concerning conspirators who do confeder or bind themselves by oath, covenant, or other alliance, as relates or extends to combinations or conspiracies of workmen or other persons to obtain an advance of or to fix the rate of wages, or to lessen or alter the hours of duration of the time of working, or to decrease the quantity of work, or to regulate or control the mode of carrying on any manufacture, trade, or business, or the management thereof, or to combinations or conspiracies of masters, manufacturers, or other persons, to lower or fix the rate of wages, or to increase or alter the hours of duration of the time of working, or to increase the quantity of work, or to regulate or control the mode of carrying on any manufacture, trade, or business, or the management thereof, or to oblige workmen to enter into work. It then repeals 3 H. 6. c. I ; 33 H. 8. st. I. c. 9. (Irish) ; 2 & 3. Ed. 6. c. 15 ; 5 Parl. Jac. I. (Scotch); 7 Parl. Jac. I. (Scotch) , 5 Parl. Mary (Scotch) ; 7 Parl. Jac. 6. (Scotch) ; 13 & 14 C. 2. c. 15. in part; 7 G. I. st. I. c. 13. in part ; 12 G. I. c. 34. in part; 3 G. 2. c. 14. (Irish) in part ; 17 G. 2. c. 28. (Irish) in part ; 22 G. 2. c. 27. in part ; 29 G. 2. c. 23. in part; 3 G. 3. c. 17. (Irish) in part; 3 G. 3. c. 34. (Irish) in part ; 8 G. 3. c. 17; 11 & 12 G. 3. c. 18 (Irish) ; 11 & 12 G. 3. c. 33. (Irish) in part ; 13 G. 3. c. 68. in part; 17 G. 3. c. 55. in part; 19 & 20 G. 3. c. 19. (Irish) in part ; 19 & 20 G. 3. c. 24. (Irish) in part; 19 & 20 G. 3. c. 36. (Irish) in part; 25 G. 3. c. 48. (Irish) in part; 32 G. 3. c. 44. in part; 36 G. 3. c. 111.; 39 G. 3. c. 56, in part; 39 & 40 G. 3. c. 106. in part; 43 G. 3. c. 86. in part ; 47 G. 3. s. 1. c. 43; 57

Certain Acts shall stand and remain repealed, viz.

33 Edw. I. so far as relates to combination of workmen.

G. 3. c. 122. in part ; and all enactments in any passing other statutes or Acts which, immediately before the relative to com- passing of the said recited Act of the last session of workmen or Parliament, were in force throughout or in any part of masters as to the United Kingdom of Great Britain and Ireland, wages, time of relative to combinations to obtain an advance of wages, quantity of or to lessen or alter the hours of duration of the time of work, &c. working, or to decrease the quantity of work, or to regulate or control the mode of carrying on any manufacture, trade, or business, or the management thereof, or relative to combinations to lower the rate of wages, or to increase the quantity of work, or to regulate or control the mode of carrying on any manufacture, trade, or business, or the management thereof, or relative to fixing the amount of the wages of labour, or relative to the obliging workmen not hired to enter into work, and every enactment enforcing or extending the application of any of the said several enactments so repealed, shall, notwithstanding the repeal of the said recited Act of the last session of Parliament, still be and remain repealed, except only so far as the same or any of them may have repealed any former Act or enactment.

III. And be it further enacted, that from and after the passing of this Act, if any person shall by violence to the person or property, or by threats or intimidation, or by molesting or in any way obstructing another, force or endeavour to force any journeyman, manufacturer, workman, or other person hired or employed in any manufacture, trade, or business, to depart from his hiring, employment, or work, or to return his work before the same shall be finished, or prevent or endeavour to prevent any journeyman, manufacturer, workman, or other person not being hired or employed from hiring himself to, or from accepting work or employment from any person or persons ; or if any person shall use or employ violence to the person or property of another, or threats or intimidation, or shall molest or in any way obstruct another for the purpose of forcing or inducing such person to belong to any club or association, or to contribute to any common

And all Acts relative to combination of workmen or masters as to wages, time of working, or quantity of work, &c.

Penalty on persons compelling journeymen to leave their employment or to return work unfinished ;

or preventing their hiring themselves ;

or compelling them to belong to clubs, &c.;

or to pay any Fines, for not having complied with orders as to wages ;

fund, or to pay any fine or penalty, or on account of his not belonging to any particular club or association, or not having contributed or having refused to contribute to any common fund, or to pay any fine or penalty or on account of his not having complied or of his refusing to comply with any rules, orders, resolutions, or regulations made to obtain an advance or to reduce the rate of wages, or to lessen or alter the hours of working, or to decrease or alter the quantity of work, or to regulate the mode of carrying on any manufacture, trade, or business, or the management thereof ;

or compelling any Manufacturer, &c. to alter his mode of carrying on business,

or if any person shall by violence to the person or property of another, or by threats or intimidation, or by molesting or in any way obstructing another, force or endeavour to force any manufacturer or person carrying on any trade or business, to make any alteration in his mode of regulating, managing, conducting, or carrying on such manufacture, trade, or business, or to limit the number of his apprentices, or the

Imprisonment, or imprisonment with hard labour for three months.

number or description of his journeymen, workmen, or servants ; every person so offending, or aiding, abetting, or assisting therein, being convicted thereof in manner herein-after mentioned, shall be imprisoned only, or shall and may be imprisoned and kept to hard labour, for any time not exceeding three calendar months.

Not to affect meetings for settling rates of wages to be received, or hours of work to be employed by the persons meeting.

IV. Provided always, and be it enacted, that this Act shall not extend to subject any persons to punishment, who shall meet together for the sole purpose of consulting upon and determining the rate of wages or prices, which the persons present at such meeting or any of them, shall require or demand for his or their work, or the hours or time for which he or they shall work, in any manufacture, trade, or business, or who shall enter into any agreement, verbal or written, among themselves, for the purpose of fixing the rate of wages or prices which the parties entering into such agreement, or any of them, shall require or demand for his or their work, or the hours of time for which he or they will work, in any manufacture, trade or business ; and that persons so meeting for the purposes aforesaid, or entering into any such agreement as aforesaid, shall not be liable to any prosecution or penalty for so doing; any law or statute to the contrary notwithstanding.

V. Provided also, and be it further enacted, that this act shall not extend to subject any persons to punishment who shall meet together for the sole purpose of consulting upon and determining the rate of wages or prices which the persons present at such meeting, or any of them, shall pay to his or their journeymen, workmen, or servants, for their work, or the hours or time of working in any manufacture, trade, or business, or who shall enter into any agreement, verbal or written among themselves, for the purpose of fixing the rate of wages or prices, which the parties entering into such agreement, or any of them, shall pay to his or their journeymen, workmen, or servants, for their work, or the hours or time of working in any manufacture, trade, or business; and that persons so meeting for the purposes aforesaid, or entering into any such agreement as aforesaid, shall not be liable to any prosecution or penalty for so doing, any law or statute to the contrary notwithstanding. *Not to affect meetings for rates of wages, &c. to be paid by masters to journeymen, &c.*

VI. And be it further enacted, that all and every persons and person who shall or may offend against this Act, shall and may, equally with all other persons, be called upon and compelled to give his or her testimony and evidence as a witness or witnesses on behalf of his majesty, or of the prosecutor or informer, upon any information to be made or exhibited under this Act, against any other person or persons not being such witness or witnesses as aforesaid; and that in all such cases every person having given his or her testimony or evidence as aforesaid, shall be and is hereby indemnified of, from, and against any information to be laid, or prosecution to be commenced against him or her, for having offended in the matter wherein or relative to which he, she, or they shall have given testimony or evidence as aforesaid. *Offenders compelled to give evidence. Indemnified.*

VII. And for the more effectually enforcing and carrying into execution the provisions of this act, be *Justices may summon offenders.*

it further enacted, that on complaint and information on oath before any one or more justice or justices of the peace, of any offence having been committed against this Act, within his or their respective jurisdictions, and within six calendar months before such complaint or information shall be made, such justice or justices are hereby authorized and required to summon the person or persons charged with being an offender or offenders against this Act, to appear before any two such justices, at a certain time or place to be specified ; and if any person or persons so summoned shall not appear according to such summons, then such justices, (proof on oath having been first made before them of the due service of such summons upon such person or persons, by delivering the same to him or them personally, or leaving the same at his or their usual place of abode, provided the same shall be so left twenty-four hours at least before the time which shall be appointed to attend the said justices upon such summons) shall make and issue their warrant or warrants for apprehending the person or persons so summoned, and not appearing as aforesaid, and bringing him or them before such justices ; or it shall be lawful for such justices, if they shall think fit, without issuing any previous summons, and instead of issuing the same, upon such complaint and information as aforesaid, to make and issue their warrants for apprehending the person or persons by such information charged to have offended against this Act, and bringing him or them before such justices ; and upon the person or persons complained against appearing upon such summons, or being brought by virtue of such warrant and warrants before such justices, or upon proof on oath of such person or persons absconding, so that such warrant or warrants cannot be executed, then such justices shall and they are hereby authorized and required forthwith to make inquiry touching the matters complained of, and to examine into the same by the oath or oaths of any one or more credible person or persons as shall be requisite, and to hear and determine the

Not appearing, warrants may be issued.

On their appearance, or proof of absconding.

Proceedings

matter of every such complaint ; and upon confession by the party, or proof by one or more credible witness or witnesses upon oath, to convict or acquit the party or parties against whom complaint shall have been made as aforesaid.

VIII. And be it further enacted, that it shall be lawful for the justices of the peace before whom any such complaint and information shall be made as aforesaid, and they are hereby authorized and required, at the request in writing of any of the parties, to issue his or their summons to any witness or witnesses to appear and give evidence before such justices, at the time and place appointed for hearing and determining such complaint, and which time and place shall be specified in such summons ; and if any person or persons so summoned to appear as a witness or witnesses as aforesaid, shall not appear before such justices, at the time and place specified in such summons, or offer some reasonable excuse for the default, or appearing according to such summons, shall not submit to be examined as a witness or witnesses, and give his or their evidence before such justices, touching the matter of such complaint, then and in every such case it shall be lawful for such justices, and they are hereby authorized (proof on oath, in the case of any person not appearing according to such summons, having been first made before such justices of the peace, of the due service of such summons on every such person, by delivering the same to him or her, or by leaving the same twenty-four hours before the time appointed for such person to appear before such justices, at the usual place of abode of such person,) by warrant under the hands of such justices, to commit such person or persons so making default in appearing, or appearing and refusing to give evidence, to some prison within the jurisdiction of such justices, there to remain without bail or mainprize, for three calendar months, or until such person or persons shall submit to be examined and give evidence before such justices as aforesaid.

Justices may summon witnesses.

Non-appearance, &c.

Proceedings.

F

Form of con-
victions and
commitments,
set forth in
schedule an-
nexed.

IX. And be it further enacted, that the justices before whom any person or persons shall be convicted of any offence against this Act, or by whom any person shall be committed to prison for not appearing as a witness, or not submitting to be examined, shall cause all such convictions, and warrants or orders for such commitments, to be drawn up in the form to the effect set forth in the schedule to this Act annexed.

Convictions
to be trans-
mitted to the
next general or
quarter sessions
to be filed.

X. And be it further enacted, that the justices before whom any such conviction shall be had, shall cause the same (drawn up in the form or to the effect herein-before directed) to be fairly written on parchment, and transmitted to the next general sessions or general quarter sessions of the peace to be holden for the county, riding, division, city, liberty, town, or place wherein such a conviction was had, to be filed amongst the records of the general sessions or general quarter sessions ; and in case any person or persons shall appeal, in manner herein-after mentioned, from the judgment of the said justices, to the said general sessions or general quarter sessions, the justices in such general sessions or general quarter sessions are hereby required, upon receiving such conviction, to proceed to the hearing and determination of the matter of the said appeal, according to the directions of this Act.

Proceedings
under this act
in Scotland.

XI. Provided always, and be it enacted, that in Scotland all prosecutions under this Act may be insisted on at the instance of the public prosecutor, and may be judged of, either by two justices of the peace, or by the sheriff of the county within which the offence may have been committed.

Persons
thinking them-
selves aggriev-
ed may appeal
to the general
or quarter ses-
sions.

XII. Provided always, and be it further enacted, that if any person convicted of any offence or offences punishable by this Act, shall think himself or herself aggrieved by the judgment of such justices, before whom he or she shall have been convicted, such person shall have liberty to appeal from every such conviction to the next court of general sessions or general quarter sessions of the peace which shall be held for the county, riding, division, city, liberty, town, or place wherein such offence was committed ; and that the execution of every judgment so appealed from shall be suspended, in case the person so convicted shall immediately enter into recognizances before such justices (which they are hereby authorised and required to take) himself in the penal sum of ten pounds, with two sufficient sureties in the penal sum of ten pounds of lawful money of Great Britain, upon condition to prosecute such appeal with effect, and to be forthcoming to abide the judgment and determination of the said next general sessions or general quarter sessions, and to pay such costs as the said court shall award on such occasion ; and the justices in the said next court of general sessions or general quarter sessions are hereby authorized and required to hear and determine the matter of the said appeal, and to award such costs as to them shall appear just and reasonable to be paid by either party, which decision shall be final ; and if upon hearing the said appeal, the judgment of the justices before whom the appellant shall have been convicted shall be affirmed, such appellant shall immediately be committed by the said court to the common gaol or house of correction, without bail or mainprize, according to such conviction, and for the space of time therein mentioned.

XIII. Provided also, and be it further enacted, that no justice of the peace, being also a master in the particular trade or manufacture, in or concerning which any offence is charged to have been committed under this Act, shall act as such justice under this Act.

No master to act as justice.

SCHEDULE TO WHICH THIS ACT REFERS.

FORM OF CONVICTION AND COMMITMENT.

Be it remembered, that on the   day of
in the   year of his majesty's
reign, and in the year of our Lord
A. B. is convicted before us (naming the justices) two
of his majesty's justices of the peace for the county,
[or riding, division, city, liberty, town, or place] of
of having [stating the offence]
contrary to the Act made in the sixth year of the
reign of King George the Fourth, intituled an Act [here
set forth the title of this Act,] and we the said justices
do hereby order and adjudge the said A. B. for the
said offence to be committed to and confined in the
common gaol for the said county, [or riding, division,
city, liberty, town, or place] for the space of
or to be committed to the house of correction
at   within the said county, [or riding,
division, city, liberty, town, or place,] there to be
kept to hard labour for the space of
given under our hands, the day and year above
written.

FORM OF COMMITMENT OF A PERSON SUMMONED AS A WITNESS.

Whereas C. D. hath been duly summoned to appear
and give evidence before us [naming the justices who
issued the summons] two of his majesty's justices of the
peace for the county [or riding, division, city, liberty,
town, or place] of   on this
day of   at   being the time

and place appointed for hearing and determining the complaint made by [the informer or prosecutor] before us, against A. B. of having [stating the offence as laid in the information] contrary to the Act made in the sixth year of the reign of king George the Fourth, intituled an Act (here insert the title of this Act :) and whereas the said C. D. hath not appeared before us, at the time and place aforesaid, specified for that purpose, or offered any reasonable excuse for his (or her) default, (or and whereas the said C. D. having appeared before us, at the time and place aforesaid, specified for that purpose, hath not submitted to be examined as a witness and give his (or her) evidence before us touching the matter of the said complaint, but hath refused so to do ;) therefore we, the said justices, do hereby in pursuance of the said statute commit the said C. D. to the [describing the prison,] there to remain without bail or mainprize, for his [or her] contempt aforesaid, for three calendar months, or until he [or she] shall submit himself [or herself] to be examined, and give his [or her] evidence before us, touching the matter of the said complaint, or shall otherwise be discharged by due course of law : and you [the constable or other peace officer or officers to whom the warrant is directed] are hereby authorized and required to take into your custody the body of the said C. D. and him [or her] safely to convey to the said prison, and him [or her] there to deliver to the gaoler or keeper thereof, who is hereby authorized and required to receive into his custody the body of the said C. D. and him [or her] safely to detain and keep, pursuant to this commitment. Given under our hands, this   day of   in the year of our Lord

[This commitment to be directed to the proper peace officer, and the gaoler or keeper of the prison.]

Dublin : Printed by JOHN S. FOLDS, 5, Bachelor's-Walk.

AN INQUIRY

INTO THE

ORIGIN, PROGRESS, AND RESULTS OF THE
STRIKE OF THE OPERATIVE COTTON
SPINNERS OF PRESTON,

FROM OCTOBER, 1836, TO FEBRUARY, 1837.

READ AT LIVERPOOL, BEFORE THE STATISTICAL SECTION OF
THE BRITISH ASSOCIATION, SEPT. 14, 1837.

BY HENRY ASHWORTH.

MANCHESTER:

PRINTED BY JOHN HARRISON, MARKET STREET.

1838.

AN INQUIRY INTO THE ORIGIN, PROGRESS, AND RESULTS OF THE STRIKE OF THE OPERATIVE COTTON SPINNERS OF PRESTON, FROM OCTOBER 1836, TO FEBRUARY 1837,

READ AT LIVERPOOL, BEFORE THE STATISTICAL SECTION OF THE BRITISH ASSOCIATION.—SEPT. 14TH, 1837.

BY HENRY ASHWORTH, ESQ.

PRESTON has, from an early period, been a principal seat of the Cotton Manufacture. In October last, there were in Preston and its vicinity, forty-two Cotton Mills, giving employment to 8500 hands, and requiring about 1200 horse power to work them; consuming about one twenty-first part of the Cotton spun in the United Kingdom; and having a capital invested in them, in buildings, machinery, &c. &c., of about ....£550,000 ; and a working capital employed, of about 250,000,

Making a total of ......£800,000.

The number of operative Spinners employed in these mills were 660,—each Spinner having under his care, on an average, about 600 spindles.

A

The year 1836 was remarkable for great activity in the Cotton Trade ; the Master Spinners were making considerable profits, or at least, such was the general belief ; and the Operative Spinners were persuaded, with some truth, that they were not sharing in the general prosperity, in the same degree as others of the same class in the neighbouring towns. Their nett earnings, that is what remained to them after paying the wages of the children employed by them as piecers, varied from 20s. to 25s. a-week, and might be averaged at 22s. 6d., which was less than was paid for the same description of work, at the same period, in other towns in the Cotton district, and particularly at Bolton, where the wages had recently been advanced and in the disputes which afterwards arose, the Bolton rate of wages was assumed as a standard, by the Operative Spinners of Preston.

It must here be observed, however, that the Preston masters had long been in the habit of adopting a uniform rate of wages, varying but little with the fluctuations in the state of their trade ; whereas, in other places, and especially at Bolton, it had been the custom for the masters to raise the wages of their work-people in favourable states of trade, and to lower them at times of depression ;—a practice which, operating in conjunction with the almost universal want of economy and forethought amongst the working class, is necessarily very detrimental to the real interests of the operatives; giving them, at one time, a strong temptation to intemperance and excess, and at another, reducing them to a very painful state of want and privation. Thus, in times of prosperity, the Bolton Operative Spinner may be receiving higher money wages than the Spinner of Preston,—but part of this difference is more nominal than real ; for, if we take into consideration the comparative cheapness of the several articles constituting the expenditure of the working man in the two towns, we shall find that the advantage is, in no small degree, in favour of Preston, so that the same money wages will go further in the latter than the former place. In Bolton, the operative pays less for his coals,—in Preston, he pays less for provisions and house rent ; and it is found that this advantage more than counterbalances the former. The disadvantage of Preston masters, in point of coals, and distance from the markets of Manchester and Liverpool, compared with Bolton, is considerable.

In October, 1836, while the Spinners of Preston were receiving, in money wages, 22s. 6d. a-week, those of Bolton were receiving about 26s. 6d.

There existed in Preston, previously to this time, a Spinners "Trades' Union," consisting of 250 to 300 members, or less than one-half of the number of Spinners employed there; but inasmuch as it was a rule, in many of the mills, to give employment to those only who were unconnected with such institutions, its acts had been chiefly confined to relieving its own sick members, or contributing to the wants of other societies.

In October, 1836, on the occasion of the Preston Spinners sending a deputation to Bolton, and other places, to inquire into the current rate of wages, the " Union" first began to assume a formidable aspect ; numerous delegates, commonly called " Agitators," began to arrive in Preston, from Bolton, and the other places visited. Meetings were held ; the disadvantages under which the Preston Spinners laboured, as compared with those of Bolton and other places, were spoken of in exaggerated terms;—the masters were denounced as unfeeling and tyrannical; and the efficacy of combinations, as a means of giving to the work-people a proper controul over the proceedings of their masters, was pointed out, and enlarged upon, with great enthusiasm.

It may be proper here to observe, that none of the Preston people were officers of the Union ;—the affairs of the Union being conducted by the delegates from other towns.

Great excitement was produced;—and nearly the whole of the Spinners, not previously members of the Union, were induced, or coerced, by threats and intimidation, to join the Union ; and under this semblance of strength, they, on the 13th of

October, appointed a Council, which commenced sitting at a public-house in the town.

The first act of the Council was, to wait on one of the most extensive houses in the town, (who were known to be very strict, in requiring from their hands an engagement not to belong to any "Trades' Union,") and demand an advance in the Spinners' wages ;—to which request the house refused to accede.

Immediately after this, six Spinners, in the employment of this house, became insubordinate, and were discharged,—the remaining Spinners threatening, thereupon, to leave their work, unless the six men were restored to work. The house in question then ascertained from their hands, that they were, in reality seeking, by the advice of the Spinners' Council, to obtain the Bolton list of prices for spinning;--the like demands being made, simultaneously, by the Spinners, to all the other masters in the town. The masters showed no disposition to give way to these demands made on them; and the result was, that all the Spinners throughout the town united in giving notice to their masters of their intention to quit their work.

The masters now held a meeting, at which it was determined to offer the Spinners an advance of ten per cent on their gross earnings, or about 3s. 4d. a-week, on the condition that they would detach themselves from the Union. This offer was, in many

instances, accepted by individual Spinners ; but the
Council of the Union, assuming the right to return
an answer, in the name of the whole body, rejected
the offer of the masters, and renewed their demand
of the " *Bolton list of prices*," unaccompanied by
any condition relative to the Union.

To these terms the masters refused to accede ;
and on Monday morning, the 7th November, the
Spinners discontinued their attendance, and the
factories were closed.

From the following statement, it would appear,
that the offer of an advance of ten per cent on the
previously existing rate of wages was, in fact, (setting
aside the question of the Union,) a concession of all
the pecuniary advance that was demanded.

Gross weekly wages of the Preston
    Spinner .... £1. 13s. 6d.
Deduct the amount of wages paid by
    the Spinner to his Piecers, ... 0 11 0

Nett weekly wages of the Spinner 1 2 6
Proposed addition of ten per cent on the
    gross amount..................... 0 3 4

The result being £1 5 10

which, taking into consideration the pecuniary advantages of cheaper living, of the Preston Spinners,
as compared with those of Bolton, was fully equal

to the 26s. 6d. earned by the latter. From this it would appear, that the struggle on the part of the operatives was rather to establish a precedent of successful resistance to the master, than to obtain any real or tangible benefit; inasmuch as the demand for the " Bolton list of prices," insisted upon by the operatives, amounted only to a difference in the mode of reckoning the amount of wages for the work performed, which at Preston is computed by the yard, and at Bolton, by the pound.

The operatives of Preston ceased working; and at the time of the turn-out, the 5th of November, they amounted, as has been stated, to 8,500 persons. Of these, 660 were Spinners.

.... 1320 were Piecers, children employed by the Spinners.

.... 6100 were Card-room hands, Reelers and Power Loom Weavers;

and 420 were Overlookers, Packers, Engineers, &c.

Total   8500

Of this number, it may be said, that only 660 (that is the whole of the Spinners,) voluntarily left their work; the greater part of the remaining 7840 being thereby thrown out of employment.

During the first fortnight of the turn-out, no change was apparent in the condition of the work-people. Some meetings were held, both by masters and men, but nothing resulted from them. At the commencement of the second fortnight, complaints began to be heard from the Card-room hands, and from the shopkeepers of the town.

Early in December, when the mills had been closed for a month, the streets began to be crowded with beggars,—the offices of the overseer were besieged with applicants for relief,—the inmates of the workhouse began to increase rapidly, and scenes of the greatest misery and wretchedness were of constant occurrence. At this period, the Spinners were receiving from the funds of the Union five-shilling a-week each, and the Piecers, some two, and others three-shillings a-week. The Card-room hands, and Power Loom Weavers were destitute of all means of support, receiving no assistance, but such as the masters afforded them, which, except in the cases of 18 or 20 individuals, who had not joined the Union, extended only to one meal a day for each person.

In December, £100. was granted by the Corporation, towards relieving the general distress, and a meeting was convened for the purpose of raising a further sum, and of considering the most effectual means of putting an end to the turn-out; but nothing resulted from it.

Towards the middle of December, when the turn-out had lasted six weeks, it was evident that the funds of the Union were nearly exhausted.

By the end of December, the distress had become universal and intense, and the masters came to the resolution of opening their mills, in order to give those who wished for it, an opportunity of resuming their work. In doing so, they announced their determination to abide by their former offer of an increase of ten per cent in the rate of wages ; but to require from all those who should enter the mills, a written declaration, to the effect that they would not, at any future time, whilst in their service, become members of any Union or combination of workmen. Immediately on the re-opening of the mills, which took place on the 9th of January, all the Card-room hands rushed anxiously to their work, but the continued absence of the Spinners, rendered it impossible to give them employment.

At the end of the first week after the mills had been opened, forty Spinners were at work, of whom eighteen were those who, as before stated, had not joined the Union, and the remaining twenty-two had never before been regularly employed in that kind of work.

In the course of the second week, the number had increased to 100, of whom some were entirely new to the work, and three were seceders from the Union ; and at the end of the third week, there were 140 Spinners at work, some of the additional 40 having been procured from neighbouring towns. Besides this, in two of the factories, a few self-acting mules, or spinning machines were substituted for common mules, thereby dispensing with the services of the Spinners.

As the number of the Spinners increased, of course a corresponding increase took place in the number of persons employed in the other departments.

Towards the middle of the fourth week, the supplies from the funds of the Union suddenly stopped, and those who had depended entirely on this resource, had no alternative left, but to endeavour to obtain re-admission into the factories.

On the 5th February, exactly three months from the day on which the mills were first closed, work was resumed in all the mills, to its usual extent ;— but about **200** of the Spinners, who had been most active in the turn-out, were replaced by new hands, and have since, either left the town, or remain there without employment.

No systematic acts of violence, or violations of the law took place, during the turn-out. Detachments of military were stationed in the town, to preserve order, but their services were not required. Some inflammatory hand-bills appeared on the walls, but without creating much sensation.

While the turn-out lasted, the operatives generally wandered about the streets, without any definite object :—seventy-five persons were brought before the magistrates, and convicted of drunkenness and disorderly conduct;—twelve were imprisoned or held to bail, for assaults or intimidation ;—about twenty young females became prostitutes, of whom more than one half are still so;—and of whom two have since been transported for theft ;—three persons are believed to have died of starvation;—not less than 5000 must have suffered long and severely from hunger and cold;—and in almost every family, the greater part of the wearing apparel and household furniture was pawned. In nine houses out of ten, considerable arrears of rent were due ;—and out of the sum of £1600. deposited in the Savings' Bank, by about sixty Spinners or Overlookers, £900. was withdrawn in the course of the three months;—and most of those who could obtain credit got into debt with the shopkeepers. The trade of the town suffered severely,—many of the small shopkeepers were nearly ruined, and a few completely so.

The following estimate has been made of the direct pecuniary loss to all classes of Operatives, in consequence of the turn-out:—

The wages of the 660 Spinners, for thirteen weeks, at 22s. 6d......	9652	0	0
The wages of 1320 Piecers, at 5s. 6d.	4719	0	0
The wages of 6520 Card-room hands, Weavers, Overlookers, Engineers, &c. averaging 9s...............	38142	0	0

Estimated loss sustained by Hand-
loom Weavers, in consequence of
the turn-out................. 9500 0 0
Estimated loss sustained by Clerks,
Waggoners, Carters, Mechanics,
Dressers, Sizers, &c., in consequence of the turn-out 8000 0 0

Total..........£70,013 0 0

From which must be deducted.

Estimated amount of
wages earned du-
ring the partial re-
sumption of work,
between the 9th
January and the 5th
February 5013 0 0
Estimated value of re-
lief given by the
masters 1000 0 0
Other private charity
and parish Relief.. 2500 0 0
Allowance to the Spin-
ners and Piecers,
from the funds of
the Union........ 4290 0 0

£12,803 0 0

Leaving a nett pecuniary loss to the
whole body of the Preston operatives of £57,210 0 0
The loss to the Masters, (being three
months' interest of £800,000 ;—
injury suffered by the machinery
standing idle ;—wages of hands
necessarily employed in taking
care of it) has been estimated at 45,000 0 0
And the loss sustained by the Shopkeepers, from loss of business and
bad debts, &c. &c............. 4,986 0 0

Making the total loss to the Town
and Trade of Preston, in this un-
availing struggle £107,196 0 0

---

* But to the town at large, it may be said, the loss of the whole sum of
£70,013. 0s. 0d., as the amount of the deductions are mostly of a charitable
nature.

RULES

TO BE

OBSERVED BY THE MEMBERS

OF THE

UNITED ORDER

OF

SMITHS.

"They helped every one his neighbour, and every
one said to his brother, be of good courage."

Isaiah, chap. 41, ver. 6.

DERBY:

PRINTED BY W. HORSLEY, SADLER-GATE BRIDGE

1839.

PREFACE.

As no degree of human happiness can possib'y exist without society, it is highly necessary men should unite in an association, tending to promote their mutual advantages, and contribute their utmost to its prosperity. The object of this institution is therefore to make provision for such of its members as may be rendered incapable of supporting themselves, and perhaps, numerous fam lies; how consoling, then, to every man, must the reflection be, that relief is provided for affliction and infirmity, and in some measure, provision made for his widow or friends at his decease; with this pleasing thought. he may gently glide down the stream of life, and sweetly sink into repose. The members are, therefore, earnestly requested strictly to conform to the following rules and regulations, particularly those who have, or may hereafter have, the direction of so laudable an undertaking, that they may exert their selves in such a manner as to establish this institution on a permanent foundation, consistent with brotherly love, which may lead to the general good to all who may enlist under the same banner, thereby inculcate and inspire the great principles of philanthrophy, each for all and all for each.

Mr. _____ _____

Entered the Trade and Sick

At _____

Aged _____

18

At a General Delegate Meeting, of the UNITED ORDER OF SMITHS, *held at Birmingham, June 12th. 13th, 14th, 15th, 16th, and 17th, 1837, the following resolutions were proposed and adopted:*—

GEORGE RYDER, *President.*

HENRY DYER, *Vice-President.*

Revised and Corrected at a Meeting of delegates held at Derby, May 20th, 21st. 22nd, and 23d, 1839.

LIST OF DELEGATES PRESENT.

MATTHEW COPE, SAMUEL JONES, JOHN SYMMONDS, ROBERT KNIGHT, JAMES LINACRE, DAVID HORTON, ARTHUR WATTS, JOHN ALLSOP, GEORGE RYDER, FREDERIC PROSSER.

GEORGE RYDER, PRESIDENT.

FREDERIC PROSSER, VICE-PRESIDENT,

WILLIAM ELLEBY, SECRETARY.

RULES &c.

RULE 1.

THAT the funds of this Order be raised for the purpose of relieving brothers when out of employ, and in cases of accident, superannuation, sickness, and death ; and the government of the Order in general, is confined to a Head, and District Lodges.

2.

That any person wishing to become a member of this Order, and having no bodily infirmity upon him, shall pay the following sums as his entrance fee.—From 20 to 25 years of age, ten shillings; from 25 to 30, twelve shillings; from 30 to 35, fifteen shillings; from 35 to 40, twenty-one shillings, and two shillings per month subscription, with threepence for liquor. But if any person wishes to avail himself of the advantages to be derived from the fund for Tramping, Superannuation, and Death, he shall be admitted if approved off by a majority of the members present, by paying half of the above sums, as his entrance fee; and one shilling per month subscription, and threepence for liquor. But no person to be admitted a member of the Trade only, unless he be longs to some other Sick Society, and to have nine months to pay his entrance fee.

3

Persons may be admitted to the Trade only, from the age of 40 to 45, by paying ten shillings and sixpence, as an entrance fee, to be proposed on a regular Lodge Night, and deposit the sum of two shillings and sixpence as a guarantee for his attendance within three months, (to be returned if rejected;) persons above 35 years of age, to produce their register or indenture.

4

That this Order shall consist of Forgers, Engine and Machine Makers, Whitesmiths, or Fitters-up, who are capable of earning their livelihood at any of the aforesaid branches; and any brother proposing or seconding any person, without knowing that he is in every respect a proper person, shall, on proof of the same, be fined ten shillings, to be paid in six months from the time incurred; the proposer's and seconder's name to be inserted in a book kept by the secretary for that purpose. Any brother coming to the lodge in a state of intoxication, so as to impede the business or harmony of the meeting, shall be requested by the president to retire; if he refuse so to do, he shall be fined one shilling; and if he still persist in disturbing the lodge, he shall be expelled the room; and any member not attending to order when called upon by the president, shall be fined for every offence, threepence; swearing or using obscene language, sixpence; introducing a stranger without leave from the president, one shilling; striking a brother at any time or place, five shillings; any brother entering into either religious, or political discussions, during lodge hours, shall be fined two shillings and sixpence. All fines to be added to the general fund.

5.

The following officers are the sole guardians of each lodge, viz.—President, Vice President, Junior Steward, and Senior Steward, to be chosen by ballot, and to remain in office six months; the vice-president to succeed the president every three months; but no person to hold any principal office until he shall have been a subscriber twelve months, and not to be re-chosen under six months, if others are eligible to serve: to be named and chosen by the members of each lodge, and to pay a fine of two shillings and sixpence for refusing to serve when legally appointed.

6.

The committee of each lodge shall consist of four brothers, (with the four principal officers and secretary) to be chosen every six months; any brother refusing to serve on the committee, shall be fined one shilling and sixpence. The committee to settle all disputes that these articles cannot determine, five of the committee to constitute a quorum; the D. G. and M. M. to be appointed in like manner, and subject to the same fines.

7.

That any officer or committee-man neglecting to attend within a quarter of an hour of the time appointed, shall be fined threepence, half an hour, sixpence; if absent the whole night, one shilling : each lodge to have the power of fixing their own day and hour of meeting and closing, (such law to be binding) but recommend it to be the first Saturday or Monday in each month.

8.

That the secretary shall be chosen annually by a majority of the members, on the May lodge night, who shall keep a correct account of all monies received and paid, summon for arrears within eight days of their becoming due, and shall receive twopence from each member whom he is obliged to summons ; likewise to inform the officers of their appointments, within the same time, or be fined one shilling for each omission. He shall report every lodge-night, at the commencement of business, the receipts, and expenditure, and read all letters received since the previous lodge-night, summons all meetings when they are necessary, enter all proceedings of general or committee meetings, in the book kept for that purpose, which shall be signed by the president and secretary at the conclusion of the meeting. The secretary to receive from the fund three pence for each member on the books each quarterly night, as a recompence for his duties Should the secretary leave the town for any length of time, he shall leave the president his key, books, &c. or be fined ten shillings.

9.

Any member neglecting to pay all his subscription and fines every monthly night, shall be fined one halfpenny for every shilling that he may leave on the book, and any member that shall be in arrears to the amount of four-shillings for the trade or eight shillings for both shall be deprived of all benefits and summoned by the secretary, and if not paid when it shall amount to eight shillings to trade, or fourteen shillings to both, such member shall be excluded: he may again be admitted by paying all arrears, provided there be a majority of members then present in his favour. Any member falling sick or lame that is suspended from the benefits, shall not be entitled to any relief until he shall have been in compliance six months. All members that are sick or out of employ, or living, or working three miles from the town where such lodge is held, to be exempt from fines for non-payment or not holding office.

10

That any member when he is sick or lame, so as to be unable to follow his employment, and has paid all demands for the space of one year, shall, upon producing a certificate from a surgeon, stating the nature of his complaint, and that the same was not occasioned by his own misconduct, receive as follows—ten shillings per week for twelve weeks; for the next twelve weeks, six shillings; and four shillings per week as long as his indisposition shall continue; his pay may commence three days previous to the doctor's certificate being received. Any member declaring off the fund, in order to avoid any reduction in his pay, or found doing any kind of work (except what his medical attendant will allow as healthful exercise) during the time he is receiving sick allowance, shall be excluded; or if he is found intoxicated, or in the street after nine o clock in the evening, during the six months from April to September inclusive, or after seven o'clock from October to March inclusive, shall be stopped one week's pay.

11

That any brother wishing to leave his situ
ation, shall give notice to the secretary, a week
previous to his leaving ; but if obliged to leave
without notice, shall give notice of the same
within twelve hours after, (except he is at a
distance of more than three miles from the
town where such lodge is held, when on such
occasions, he shall have eighteen hours allowed) or be fined two shillings. Any brothre
leaving his shop, through his own misconduct,
shall not be entitled to any benefit; and any
secretary or relieving officer, knowingly granting weekly allowance, or giving a card to any
brother, who is not entitled to the same, shall
be fined ten shillings and sixpence—the secretary, in cases of difficulty, to appeal to the president or committee.

12

Any brother hearing of a vacancy in any
shop, shall inform the secretary or relieving
officer, within twenty-four hours, or be fined
two shillings and sixpence, except inevitable
business detain him from so doing; the relieving officer to inform the first that applies to him
(if qualified) without delay, or be fined the

same sum; any person getting a situation from such information, shall he fined the same sum, if he neglect to inform the secretary within twelve hours after getting such situation The relieving officer to give in a report of all such cases each monthly night; and any brotherprocuring a shop for any person not a member, when a member wants employment, and is qualified to accept it, shall be fined ten shillings.

13

When any member shall have just occasion to leave his employ, and shall have paid all demands for the space of six months, he shall receive the pass-word, and a cheque card, acknowledging him to belong to the Order, with beds and beer agreeable to rule. (see index.) If one year a member, he becomes free, and shall receive weekly allowance, beds and beer, and one halfpenny per mile; if two years a member, allowance according to rule, and one penny per mile, and one shilling and sixpence and bed for sunday. No brother to be allowed to leave the town where he may have been at work, without leave from the officers, but on no occasion shall a brother pass a lodge at which he is entitled to relief, upon pain of forfeiture of his relief at the lodge at which he applies. No brother to be relieved twice from the same lodge within six months. The weeks pay to be considered as relief; the branch of trade to be inserted in each card given out.

14

Any member meeting with any accident so as ever after to disable him from following his employment, providing the accident did not occur through intoxication, or was not caused by improper conduct, shall receive the sum of one shilling from each member in the order; such person to be allowed to remain a member, by paying threepence per month, but to be one year before he be entitled to funeral allowance from the time of receiving the donation, and not be entitled to any other privilege.

15

That no member shall receive relief from the sick and trade at the same time.

16

That each lodge of this Order be provided with a list of all fines, included in the articles, to be placed in a conspicuous part of the lodge room, by the president, on each night of meet-

ing, the president to be fined sixpence for neglecting the same.

17

That any member neglecting to attend general or monthly meetings by the time specified
in the summons, shall be fined sixpence; and
any secretary neglecting to summon such meeting, when requested by the president or committee, shall be fined two-pence for every member he may have omitted to summon, if such
member is within the limits.   Stewards that
shall neglect to visit each sick member that is
on the lodge, (at least once a week) shall be
fined six pence for every omission. New members that may have paid all their entrance and
subscriptions, shall be allowed to vote on all
occasions.

18

That any member divulging any of the
transactions of the Order to any person not a
member, be fined five shillings; any member
upbraiding a brother member with having received relief from the Order, be fined five
shillings.

18

19

That there shall be two auditors appointed, who shall examine the lodge books every six months, to be chosen by ballot, on the April and October meetings, aud shall meet the four principal officers and secretary, within six days after the lodge night; after the books are examined, the auditors' report shall be entered into the minute book, and read to the members on the following lodge night, by the president or one that he may appoint, or be fined; (see index) the officers and auditors to be allowed one pint of beer from the funds of the order.

20

That there be a register book kept by the secretary of each lodge, wherein each brother's name, residence, and employ, shall be inserted, and any brother moving from either, shall inform the secretary the following lodge-night, or be fined sixpence for every offence : and each relieving officer, or secretary, shall have a book for the purpose of keeping a correct account of the applications and situations that may be forwarded to him ; and should any officer lose such book, he shall make it good himself.

21

That every lodge of the Unity shall keep a general register, wherein each brother's name, the branch of trade he may follow, and the lodge he entered, shall be inserted; and any member of this order having business to transact with the relieving officer, shall call at his residence, and in no case at the works where he is employed : the residence of the relieving officers to be left at the lodge-house, any brother not acting in accordance with this rule, shall be fined two shillings.

22

Any member attempting to break up or encourage the breaking up of this order, the same being satisfactorily proved, shall be fined one guinea, or for ever excluded. Any member found guilty of imposing, or knowingly suffering others so to do, embezzling any part of the society's stock, the same being fairly proved to the committee, such offending brother shall be excluded. And should any brother undermine another in his shop, in order to take his situation, if proved to the satisfaction of the same, to be fined a sum not less than one guinea, or be excluded.

23

That each lodge shall have an anniversary dinner, but that it be left optional on what day they hold it, but recommend that it be held near as possible to the first Monday in July. No portion of the orders' funds to be applied to the payment of the dinner or any other expenses connected with it; every member if he is working or resides within the space of five miles from the town, should pay two shillings, and if within ten miles, one shilling, if more than ten miles to be exempt; and all that attend, to be clean and sober, or be fined two shillings and sixpence.

24

That any member getting in debt with the landlord, the Order shall not be answerable for it, and any secretary neglecting to inform the landlord of such law, shall be fined five shillings.

25

That each Lodge shall appoint a treasurer who shall give them a proper security for all cash and other property that he may be entrusted with.

26

Any member who shall have arrived at the age of 65 years, and shall have paid into this society 40 years, he shall for the remainder of his life, receive the weekly sum of three shillings; if 65, and shall have paid 35 years, he shall receive the weekly sum of two shillings and sixpence; if 65, and shall have paid 30 years, he shall receive two shillings; and if arrived at 70, and paid in 30 years, he shall receive the sum of two shillings per week for the remainder of his life.

SUPERANNUATION TABLE.

Paid all demands for years.	Arrived at the age of years.	To receive per week as superannuation
40	65	3s. 0d.
35	65	2s. 6d.
30	65	2s. 0d.
30	70	2s. 0d.

27

At the death of a free member, his widow
or representative shall receive as follows.—if
the member entered under 30 years of age, for
the first year, £4. and £1. for each following
year, until it amounts to £8.; from 30 to 35
years, £3., and £1. for each year that he may
have been free, until it amounts to £8.; from
35 to 40 years, £2. for the first year, and one
for each succeeding year, until it amounts to
£7. Each member shall receive at the death
of his wife, half the sum that she herself is entitled to at his decease. Those belonging to
the trade only, to be entitled to half the allowance as mentioned above.

28

The duty of each district lodge shall be to
communicate with the several branches, and
the head lodge, order remittances of cash when
necessary, and see that their respective lodges
are conducted in a proper manner; and where
there is a possible chance of establishing a
lodge, that they may be empowered to send a
person for that purpose; and that a meeting of
delegates from each district lodge take place
once every three years, but that a majority of

the district lodges be empowered to call one oftener, if necessary business should require it; (in case of equal numbers, the head lodge to have the casting vote,) and each delegate meeting to name the time and place of the succeeding one.

29

The head corresponding secretary to receive fifteen shillings per quarter, and the corresponding secretary of each district lodge to have two shillings per quarter extra, for their services and one pint of ale for the relief of each tramp.

30

That there shall be three auditors appointed annually, to examine the whole accounts of the Unity, and shall meet at such place as may from time to time be agreed upon, on the second Monday in May; and shall make out a proper return of the money received and paid to each person, either as weekly, tramping, sick, superannuation, or general pay; and shall see the returns printed, or put in such way, that the head secretary can have them printed ready to be returned by the thirty-first day of May. And any secretary who shall neglect to send in these accounts so that they may be received by such time, shall be fined any sum not less than ten shillings and sixpence.

That in case of the death of a member or member's wife, notice shall be immediately sent to the secretary, who shall summon the president and stewards to meet as early as possible to pay the funeral allowance; and if the deceased member should have requested, previous to his death, that he be attended at his funeral, by the committee or officers of the society, such officers shall be summoned in due time, for that purpose, by the secretary; each officer attending to be allowed sixpence; twopence to be paid by each member, at the death of a brother, and one penny at the death of a brother's wife, to be charged to his contribution the first lodge-night after the report is made out.

SCALE OF FINES FOR NON-PAYMENT

OF A MEMBER OF BOTH

SICK AND TRADE.

No. of nights.	In arrears.	Fines.
1	2s.	1d.
2	4s.	2d.
3	6s.	3d.
4	8s.	4d.
5	10s	5d.
6	12s.	6d.
7	14s.	excluded

For Trade only, half the above fines.

Name of Town	Weekly Allowance.	Beds & Beer
Derby	One Week	{ 2 beds & pint of beer
Nottingham ..	One ditto	3 beds ditto
Manchester ..	Two ditto	3 beds ditto
Liverpool	Two ditto	3 beds ditto
London	Four ditto	5 beds ditto
Northampton..	One ditto	2 beds ditto
Bedford	One ditto	2 beds ditto
Oxford	One ditto	2 beds ditto
Preston	One ditto	2 beds ditto
Kendall......	One ditto	2 beds ditto
Dumfries	One ditto	2 beds ditto
Carlisle	One ditto	2 beds ditto
Cheltenham ..	One ditto	2 beds ditto
Warrington ..	One ditto	2 beds ditto
Leamington ..	One ditto	2 beds ditto
Wolverhampton	One ditto	2 beds ditto
Bolton	One ditto	2 beds ditto
Worcester	One ditto	2 beds ditto
Chester	One ditto	2 beds ditto
Shrewsbury ..	One ditto	2 beds ditto
Darlington ..	One ditto	2 beds ditto
Gloucester ...	One ditto	2 beds ditto
Durham	One ditto	2 beds ditto
Chesterfield ..	One ditto	2 beds ditto
Sheffield	Two ditto	3 beds ditto
Leicester	One ditto	2 beds ditto

Name of Town	Weekly Allowance.	Beds & Beer
Loughborough	*One ditto*	2 *beds* *ditto*
Birmingham ..	*Two ditto*	3 *beds* *ditto*
Wrexham	*One ditto*	2 *beds* *ditto*
Banbury	*One ditto*	2 *beds* *ditto*
Marlborough	*One ditto*	2 *beds* *ditto*
Coventry	*One ditto*	2 *beds* *ditto*
Bristol	*Two ditto*	3 *beds* *ditto*
Bath	*One ditto*	2 *beds* *ditto*
Bridgewater ..	*One ditto*	2 *beds* *ditto*
Taunton	*One ditto*	2 *beds* *ditto*

LIST OF FINES.

Article.   *s.*   *d.*

4. Proposing and seconding improper
    Persons 10   0
    Disturbing the lodge when intoxicated 1   0
    Disorderly 0   3
    Swearing or obscene language.... 0   6
    Introducing strangers improperly.. 1   0
    Striking a Brother 5   0
    Improper discussions 2   6
5. Refusing to serve for principal
    Officers 2   6
6. Refusing to serve on the Committee 1   6
    The D. G. and M. M. subject to the
    same fine.
7. Officers not attending time, quarter
    of an hour 3d, half an hour 6d,
    whole night.................. 1   0
8. Secretary neglecting to summons   1   0
    Ditto   omitting to leave Keys,
Books, &c. when going out of town 10   0
10 Any Member imposing on the Sick
    funds, will be excluded; and not
    acting agreeable to the rule shall
    forfeit his week's Pay.
11. Not giving timely notice of a vacancy 2   6
    The relieving officer not giving in-
    formation of the same, agreeable
    to article 2   6

Article.	s.	d.
Neglecting to return imformation when getting employ	2	6
Procuring a shop for others when a Brother is out of employ if he be competent	10	0
16. President neglecting his duty	0	6
17. Members neglecting to attend to meetings when summoned	0	6
Secretaries neglecting to summons when required, each omission	0	2
Stewards not visiting the sick agreeable to the Rule	0	6
18. Exposing the Business of the Lodge	5	0
Upbraiding a Brother for having received relief	5	0
19. Auditors and President	1	6
20. Members neglecting to give information of residence &c.	0	6
21. Persons applying to Officer for relief when at work	2	0
22. Attempting to break up, or encourage the same	21	0
Imposing on, or embezzling the funds, excluded.		
Undermining a Brother, &c.	21	0
23. Not attending the Anniversary, 5 miles and under, 2s., 10 miles and under	1	0

Article.	*s.*	*d.*
23. Not clean and sober	2	6
24. Secretary neglecting duty to Landlord	5	0
30. Secretaries neglecting to forward their accounts to the General Auditors' Meeting	10	6

INDEX OF ARTICLES.

——0——

Derby HEAD LODGE.

DISTRICT LODGES. BRANCH LODGES.

Nottingham includes   *Leicester, Loughbro',*
                     Chesterfield, and Sheeffild

Manchester ——*Warrington and Bolton*

Liverpool ——*Chester, Shrewsbury, Wrex-*
               ham, and Preston

Carlisle ——*Darlington, Kendall, Dur-*
               ham, and Dumfries.

London ——

Northampton——*Oxford, Bedford, Leaming-*
               ton, Banbury, Marlbou-
               rough, and Coventry

Worcester ——*Gloucester, Cheltenham,*
               Birmingham, and Wolver-
               hampton

Bristol ——*Bath, Bridgewater, & Taun-*
               ton

WILLIAM HORSLEY, PRINTER, DERBY.

STATEMENT OF FACTS

CONNECTED WITH

THE TURN-OUT

IN THE

LANCASHIRE BUILDING TRADES,

WITH

COPIES OF THE PRINCIPAL DOCUMENTS

ISSUED

BY THE EMPLOYERS AND OPERATIVES;

WITH REMARKS UPON

TRADES' UNIONS AND THEIR EFFECTS.

MANCHESTER:]

PRINTED AT THE ADVERTISER AND CHRONICLE OFFICE, MARKET-STREET.

DEDICATION.

To the Employers and Operatives in the Building Trades of Lancashire, in the earnest hope that this plain and unvarnished statement of facts may tend in some degree to the restoration of that good understanding which it is the interest of both parties to maintain,

This Pamphlet is humbly dedicated,

By their well-wisher,

THE COMPILER.

Manchester,
April 2nd, 1846.

STATEMENT, &c.

The principle of association is natural to the human mind, and has prevailed in all ages. It is therefore but reasonable that we should expect to find it early applied to the operations of trading communities. The ancient guilds which prevailed over the whole of Europe, centuries ago, are a confirmation of this assertion. In the infancy of commerce the influence of these bodies did not exercise a materially detrimental effect, capital being then both small and insecure. The inadequacy of these societies to modern periods is shown by the languishing condition and desuetude into which, when they have not been subverted by authority, they have fallen. They had once their use in cherishing the early efforts of enterprise. As, however, commerce increased in strength, it was enabled to dispense with what, at an earlier period, was an assistance of some value, but which, in process of time, degenerated into a clog and an incumbrance. The Trades' Union of the present day at first sight presents some of the features of the ancient guild. A closer examination of the two dispels this idea. The latter formed a bond of union between the mployer and his workmen, uniting their interests, and generating feelings of mutual confidence These advantages are not produced by the former, which is a combination of artizans alone, the bond of whose union is opposition to the employer, suspicion of his motives, and depreciation of his authority. Let me, however, not be misunderstood in this or any subsequent remark on this point. All must acknowledge that the right to combine is one to which artizans are fully entitled. But it is essential to the general good that in exercising this right none but legitimate objects are sought, and legitimate means employed. Under proper regulations, combination is capable of producing great advantages, and supplying important deficiencies. In the application to philanthropic purposes its utility has been eminently manifest.* I will even go farther than this. I will fully admit that an association of artizans may produce advantageous results both to masters and men. The labour of the artizan is his capital, and he is justified in

---

* I allude to accident, sick, and burial societies, and others for providing the means of support for widows and orphans, although it is well known hat even these have appropriated, in opposition to their own rules, portions their funds to the support of contests with employers.

A 3

disposing of it to the greatest advantage, and protecting it from injury or depreciation. But he is justified in no more. Protection he may properly and rightfully assert for himself, and he may unite with his fellows to maintain that protection. But he must stop there. He has no right to assail or to interfere with others. He may bind himself, or a body of artizans may bind themselves, to do or not to do certain things, but they cannot insist upon strangers to their body being governed by their regulations, or bound by their restrictions. The moment this line is transgressed, that moment a complete change is effected in the character and operation of the body. From a positive good, it becomes a positive evil, and the results are dangerous in the extreme. These facts are sufficiently evidenced to every mind by reference to the origin and general operations of Trades' Unions.

Every trade presents the same results, and reads the same sad and stern lesson. The trades connected with building, the various branches of the cotton manufacture, the tailors—in a word, the annals which detail the history of every occupation to which the energies of our artizans have been at any period directed, possess records of strikes, varying indeed in length and extent, but equal in intensity wherever they have occurred. From one example you may learn all. Perhaps the strike which was the most determined, and lasted the longest, in any one town, was that of the spinners in Preston in the winter of 1836-7. The object was to obtain the " Bolton list of prices," a fluctuating scale, happening at the moment to be higher than that of Preston, though but a short period before much lower. Before a single man had left work, the masters held a meeting, and determined to offer an advance of ten per cent. on the existing rate, on condition that the men should not be connected with any union. These terms were not accepted. The hands turned out on the 7th of November, and remained out to the number of 8,500 for three months. On the 5th of February, the mills resumed full work. At wages demanded by the " council of the union?" No. It was at the ten per cent. advance, offered by the masters before a single hand ceased to work. The question which every man should ask, when he hears the orator of his club room recommending a strike against his tyrant master is this, " What is the good of it ?" There was no good gained in the Preston case. The practical result of that affair was that the men resumed work on the terms they might have obtained, and were, in point o fact, offered, without leaving their employment for an hour. But you may perhaps say, "Well, the men who struck were the only sufferers, and if it pleased them, though it failed, they had a right to do it." But they were not the only sufferers. Their wives and families were pinched as well as them, in many cases more severely. The health, aye, and the modesty and virtue of their daughters, were subjected to a trial in many cases too hard for them to bear.* The boys being prevented from employing themselves, grew up in habits of indolence, fell into loose company, and, in many instances, have dated their progress to the tread mill and the hulks from the three months' idleness of the Preston strike. Many a hard-working, careful wife (for the poor women too often have to bear the brunt of these strikes) has been weighed down for months and months by the debts to shopkeepers which she has been obliged to contract, and thus she has been obliged to deny her family comforts, and even necessaries, clothing and education, she otherwise might have afforded. The evils then of strikes do not all fall upon the heads of the movers therein. They fall upon his wife and children ; and unhappiness, ignorance, and vice, in many, far too many, cases are entailed, for no lasting, or even temporary benefit. Besides, man is only part of a community, and whatever injures himself affects others. It is as if you throw a stone into a pond ; the water is only struck in one narrow spot, but the successive circles which follow the splash show the whole pool to feel its influence. So in this case, one man cannot be thrown out of employment—that is to say, so much labour, which is capital, cannot be subtracted from circulation—without the community feeling it in some degree, however slight. How much more then when a large number of men throw themselves out. Let me call attention, once more, to the Preston affair. At the end of the second fortnight the shopkeepers began to complain. They had trusted all their stock, and could not renew it, because they had no ready money. At the month's end, the streets began to fill with beggars, and the overseer's office to be crowded with applicants for relief, and the workhouse to be positively packed. Many of the card-room and other hands (whom the absence of the spinners had deprived of employment) were supported by the bounty of the masters. By the end of December the distress became so severe that the corpo-

* It is known beyond question, that many young girls were throw upon the streets through distress ; and twenty cases were distinctly proved, in which they became confirmed in that horrid life.

ration were obliged to vote a grant of one hundred pounds towards diminishing its intensity, and the masters threw open their mills to any one who would leave the union, at the 10 per cent. advance. The first week after this, 40 persons were at work, the second, 100, and the third, 140. Some *self-acting mules* were obtained from Manchester the same week, thus dispensing with several men. In the fourth week the supplies from the funds of the union were found to have been exhausted by the council; and on the 5th of February, the mules were at full work on the terms offered three months before. Two hundred men, however, were unable to re-enter them, their places having been supplied by strangers from other towns, *and by the self-acting mules.* The town and trade of Preston, in the mean time, lost, as has been calculated, no less a sum than £107,196 ; many shopkeepers were utterly ruined; general trade was prostrated ; violence and crime in some instances committed; furniture, wearing apparel, and every thing convertible pawned or sold ; misery, destitution, sickness, and (in three cases) absolute starvation—all were borne for three whole months. And with what result ? Only at the end to be forced into accepting what was offered before a single loom was stopped—or (and this deserves thinking upon) *a single self-actor introduced.** The great turn-out in Glasgow, in the summer of 1837, presents the same result. In that case, the strike lasted 17 weeks, and the loss in wages alone (independent of every other item by which the town and trade of the place was affected) was no less than £47,600. It has also been calculated that the loss to the county of Lanark from the turn-outs of the colliers, the iron moulders, the sawyers, and the spinners, was, in the year 1843 alone, £500,000—half a million of money positively wasted, as if it had been cast into the sea.

---

* Strikes lead to the superseding of hand labour by machines. In 1831, on the occasion of a strike at Manchester, several of the capitalists, afraid of their business being driven to other countries, had recourse to the celebrated machinists, Messrs. Sharp and Co., of Manchester, requesting them to direct the inventive talents of their partner, Mr. Roberts, to the construction of a self-acting mule, in order to emancipate the trade from the impending ruin threatening it. Under assurances of the most liberal encouragement in the adoption of his invention, Mr. Roberts suspended his pursuits as an engineer, and set his fertile genius to construct a spinning automaton. In the course of a few months he produced a machine, called the " Self-acting Mule," which, in 1834, was in operation in upwards of sixty factories ; doing the work of the head spinners so much better than they could do it themselves, as to leave them no chance against it.

Besides these that I have just enumerated, other cases may be readily accumulated which prove the same facts, and lead to the same lamentable conclusions. I am afraid of detaining you too long by these preliminary observations, but I cannot, consistently with my sense of their importance, avoid noticing the cases in which the frequent occurrence of combinations, and the exorbitant demands of the unions, have caused the entire removal of a manufacture to situations which are exempt from the improper control sought to be imposed. Mr. Babbage, in his work on " Machinery and Manufactures," quotes an instance in which an extensive millowner—finding it impossible to carry on his business profitably, on account of the unjust interference of his workmen—removed his entire establishment to the United States. In Dublin at no very distant period there were several ship builders in extensive business. At the present time there is but one. The reason is to be found in the circumstance that whenever trade became brisk, an immediate attempt was made, by means of strikes, for an increase of wages. In the same city in other trades a similar result has been produced from the same cause, and it has been calculated that work to the amount of £10,000 per annum in the foundry trade alone is executed elsewhere, which would have been done there but for the effect of combinations among the workmen. The lace trade of Nottinghamshire and the silk trade of Macclesfield have each been considerably diminished in importance from the same cause.

Having thus laid before you some general results of the operations of unions in many other branches of trade, let me call your attention particularly to their effects as regards the building trades in Lancashire, the more especial object of this compilation. In the year 1833, the last great turn-out of the building trades occurred. In the commencement of that year it became known, beyond all possibility of doubt, that there existed in Manchester, Liverpool, Preston, Leeds, Huddersfield, Bradford, Bolton, and other large towns, a widely spread system of combinations among the operatives. The first exercise of authority on the part of the rulers of these bodies was to issue a code of arbitrary and dictatorial regulations, unsigned by any responsible party, creating themselves, to all intents and purposes, into a secret tribunal, before which the actions and even the sayings of the employers were canvassed and adjudicated, and decisions pronounced and edicts sent forth, tending to the subversion of the good spirit and confidence which should exist between the masters and operatives, and also between the masters and their employers, the public. Owing to the non-compliance of the masters with some of the unreasonable demands which were thus made upon them, the whole of the artizans quitted their work, and put a stop to all building operations in the towns mentioned. The object contemplated by the men, according to their own statements in their addresses to the public, was to do away with the system of contracting,—that one person should not be allowed to undertake the whole of the several branches of the trade. The masters, desirous of giving a fair trial to the proposed system (although unable to see the precise manner in which the former system could affect the wages of the operatives), declined entering into contracts, except for the different trades separately; affording thereby a proof of their desire to meet the wishes of the men. It however became evident, from the unwarrantable demands succeeding each other, that the journeymen had ulterior objects in view; and aimed at the erection of a system of dictation and interference, which should constitute the council of the union a sort of great middle-man between the employer and the employed. Concession followed concession, until the demands of the " general union" became so excessive, that further compliance was out of the question; the public no less than the masters being the sufferers. The masters at length found themselves obliged to determine to resist this combination, by declining any longer to employ men connected with the union, and in consequence a general turn-out ensued. The men struck upon the 8th of June, and remained absent from their employ till the commencement of September in the same year, when work was resumed upon the conditions originally offered by the masters.

As an illustration of the spirit of this turn-out, in Manchester and Liverpool, we subjoin the following documents, which are among the mandates issued by the Union at this period :

North British Volunteer, Deansgate, June 10th, 1833.
Sir,—You have, in the face of our established rules, of which you were furnished with a copy, so far as regards Machinery Operating on Carpentry and Joinery, and in the face of the said rules you have discharged an old and tried servant of yours for not complying with your wishes in breaking through the said rules.

This is to inform you, that we wish you to take back to your employ the person so discharged by you, and likewise to refrain from requiring any of the men in your employ to infringe on the said rule, or any other rule of ours, of which you have been furnished with a copy, otherwise the men in your employ will be under the necessity of striking ; and any expense that may occur, if you drive us to such necessity, will be required at your hands. By order of   FRIENDLY OPERATIVE JOINERS OF MANCHESTER.
For Mr. John Wallis, Mays-street.

June 1st.

Brothers,—In consequence of your Employer not complying with the resolutions of our Committee, we suspend you all from working until Mr. Leatham gives us more satisfaction than he has done. Our Committee meet on Monday evening.

Secretary of the Committee,   O. L. P.

To Brothers in Messrs. Leatham's employment.

Liverpool, June 12th, 1833,

Sir,—The Committee agree that you shall take Hugh Quinan as an Apprentice, until he is 21 years of age, providing you bind him within one fortnight from this date, and tender the Indenture to our Committee for their approval; and you are to discontinue Stringer in your employment until he becomes a member of our Society.

Committee of the   O. L. P.

To Mr. Clark, Plasterer, Nash Grove.

Samuel Holme, Esq.   Liverpool, 11th April, 1833.

Sir,—In consequence of an information received by our Society, that your job in Canning-street is a Contract job, we felt ourselves in duty bound to furnish your men at that job with a notice to that effect, and in consequence of such Contract to leave that building directly. You will please to understand that previous to their return we require to see your Contract in our club-room, to be examined by our Committee appointed for that purpose. When we receive this information, we will be happy to be, Sir, your most obedient humble servant,

The Operative Societies of Bricklayers'
Corresponding Secretary.

Direct O.L.B., George the Fourth's Head, Hood-street.
Samuel Holme, Esq., Seel-street.

John Hogan,   Liverpool, 10th June, 1833.

Sir,—From the information we have received, that you are at work at Mr. James Brancker's, for Mr. Samuel Holme, and as you are not working piece-work, we request you to knock off immediately.—We are, yours &c.,

From the Committee of Operative Bricklayers.

From the period of which we have just given a short sketch, a spirit of harmony began by degrees to develope itself, and to produce the fruits which invariably spring from it. The consequence was, that, amidst all the fluctuations which that eventful period of thirteen years, between 1833 and 1846, has beheld, from the mutual kindness and good feeling of masters and men, the building trade has suffered less and prospered more than any other which can be named. It is true, occasionally symptoms of an evil influence at work now and then manifested themselves, and it was hinted that the Unions were in course of extensive revival, not only in this, but in the neighbouring towns. As regarded Manchester, such whispers were looked upon with but little fear, for it was thought that the great concession the masters had made in the grant of the Saturday half-holiday to the carpenters and joiners would form a bond of fellowship that no external influence could rupture or endanger. The mention of the half-holiday brings me to the consideration of the question of the applicability of that arrangement to the building trades. I am eminently favourable to an abridgment of the hours of labour among all classes of artizans. In my own sphere have done all I can to help on the cause, and I have the pleasure to possess the friendship of the prime movers in the original obtainment of the very half-holiday I am now noticing. But abstractedly right as the half-holiday is, there arises a difficulty in deciding its applicability to the building trades, and I must find myself forced to the conclusion that the half-holiday is impracticable and of no avail, if it is not universal, in the building trades. It is greatly to be desired—I should wish to advise its general adoption; but until it is, as every one who will look at it rightly must see, there is a difficulty about it. The writer of a leading article in the *Manchester Advertiser* has so clearly, and at the same time briefly, expressed the grounds which have led me, equally with him, to this conclusion, that I will call your attention to his remarks, which are in these terms :—

It has been found that the half-holiday system, however desirable as a measure *fully* carried out, was most inconvenient when only *partially* applied to the building trades. The joiner is the operative who has often a kind of supervision over the other branches, when working in the country. The half-day-holiday of the carpenter has, in consequence, often proved exceedingly productive of loss to the contractor, by having the bricklayers, plasterers, painters, plumbers, glaziers, slaters, and labourers, left for half a day without the assistance and superintendence of the joiners; they being frequently required to do work at the moment, which is absolutely necessary to enable the other trades to proceed.

Such was the position of the building trades on the last day of February in this year, since which time till the day on which I now write, April 2nd, a general cessation of work has existed. I propose now to consider the causes alleged on the sides of masters and men in regard to this cessation, to produce and comment upon the documents of each party, and to suggest my own views as to the policy which should be pursued in order to procure a speedy and amicable settlement. The first document which appeared was a placard from the carpenters and joiners, which was profusely posted in the town. A copy of this I have endeavoured to obtain from the printer, and in every other quarter which seemed to me likely, but without success. I regret this, as it in some degree interferes with the completeness of this compilation. The requirements of the men, however, were to the following effect :— That the wages of each joiner should be raised from 26s. to 29s. per week, in addition, too, to the previous concessions of the masters, as regards the half holiday, &c. The masters, unwilling to accede to

13

terms which would so materially interfere with existing contracts,
made the proposal to give 28s. per week, on condition that the original
rules regarding the hours of labour should be resumed. These terms
were refused by the men, and it speedily came to the ¦knowledge of the
masters, that this was but a partial developement of an organised
system of trades' unions in their worst form. It then became imperative
upon the masters to take some measures to meet the danger by which
they were menaced, and a meeting took place, from which the following address to the public emanated :—

TO THE PUBLIC OF MANCHESTER, SALFORD, AND THEIR VICINITIES.

No. 1, Ducie Place, Exchange Buildings,
March 9th, 1846.

We, the undersigned firms, being concerned in the building trades
generally, beg leave to state to the public, that on account of the unjust
interference, and the dictatorial demands of the operatives in our employ, we
have been most reluctantly and unwillingly compelled to form ourselves into
an association for our protection, and to resist the un-English combination
that does now, and has for some time, existed amongst the operatives, and
which has been found to be very mischievous, and to interfere most un-
warrantably with the lawful and legitimate mode of carrying on our own
business ; being alike annoying to ourselves and our customers, and injurious
to the operatives themselves, and very unfortunately severing that bond of
good-will which, at all times, it is desirable should exist between the
employer and the employed.

We have no desire or intention to lower the price of labour, but to pay
a good workman good wages ; in fact, to pay according to merit, the true
standard of talent, being what the workmen themselves profess to be
regulated by.

Every operative has an undoubted right to dispose of his labour to the
best advantage ; the employer, on the other hand, has an equal right to use
the same liberty of making *his* bargain—each being free either to accept or
reject the terms offered. With these views of the case, as respects wages,
we doubt not the public will coincide with us. Our firm conviction is, that
all combination, or attempts at legislation for wages, either on the part of
masters or men, are alike unsatisfactory and injurious, in principle and
practice.

With regard to the hours of labour, we neither wish nor desire anything
beyond the old-established rules of the trade ; as, from experience, we find
that one uniform system as to time, as far as practicable, is the most satisfactory to all branches of the building trade.

We are no longer allowed to control or govern our own establishments—
the spirit of dictation assumed by the operatives forbids it. A continual
demand is made upon us, or an order is issued by a nameless committee—it
must be complied with to the letter, or a strike is the consequence. If from
the Joiners and Carpenters' Operative Association, ¸the general body of
the operatives are compelled to make the cause their own ; if from the
Labourers' Society, the effect is the same ; as well as with the bricklayers,
plumbers, plasterers, and painters, or slaters. We are neither allowed a
voice nor opinion, either as to wages, hours of labour, number of
apprentices, or labourers.

No workman, however clever at his business, or however opposed he may
conscientiously be to the trades' unions, is allowed by them to be a *legal*

man, unless he joins with and becomes one of their body; should he dare to refuse, or to pay, as in many cases, a heavy fine (which is also impose even if he consents), a strike must be made against him by all the other trades as well as his own; and he, unfortunately for himself and family, has no alternative but to comply with their imperative and tyrannical demands, or quit the town altogether (this applies equally to strangers or natives); he *must* either join their club, quit the neighbourhood, or remain and starve.

Any master not complying with the demands issued by, or emanating from, the committee of the operatives (although without signature), a strike takes place, and the offending party is not allowed to have a single man to work anywhere; if he employs any one not a member of their union, and he is sent to a job, notice is forthwith given to him that he must quit the place or building; if he does not at once comply, all the other trades turn out, no matter how important soever the work, all must stand until their laws and demands, whether made on master or man, are complied with; and it is a fact, that an offending party has been sentenced not to be allowed, what they term, a legal man for twelve months or two years. This is a state of things that we feel confident the public will neither sanction nor tolerate; we therefore, in full assurance of the justice of our cause, throw ourselves upon the indulgence of our customers, and respectfully entreat them to co-operate with us in our endeavours to manage our own affairs, and in obtaining the same freedom (in this free country), which is enjoyed by themselves in all their commercial transactions. That the cause is theirs as well as ours is obvious; we therefore trust that wherever any work may be for a while suspended, we may appeal to and have the concurrence of all lovers of impartial and even-handed justice, and confidently rely upon the forbearance of our customers, and the good-will of all architects or clerks of works, in our endeavours to maintain that freedom in the management of our affairs which is enjoyed by the rest of the community, and which, in this boasted land of freedom, is the disputable right of the meanest subject of the realm.

Ashurst John, plumber and glazier
Bellhouse David, builder
Bowden and Edwards, builders
Birch William, ditto
Brougham Matthew, ditto
Bell John, ditto
Beatson and Lawton, bricklayers
Batty John, ditto
Bowen John, ditto
Blackburn Peter, ditto
Binks William, plumber
Beardsall William, ditto
Barge John, ditto
Black Alexander, slater
Burns John, plasterer
Barrow Samuel, ditto
Bowring ——, plumber
Coulthurst and Froggatt, builders
Cairns Alexander, ditto
Clarke and Buckles, bricklayers
Carline Thomas, ditto
Cooper George, ditto
Chidgey William, ditto
Carter ——, ditto
Chadwick James, plumber
Chadfield Geo., plasterer and painter
Creik Adam, ditto, ditto

Curtis David, plasterer and painter
Christie William, slater
Dent James, plumber
Dale Thomas, builder
Duesbury William, ditto
Drewry Benjamin, ditto
Davison R. and John, ditto
Davies W. G., plumber
Dickenson Thomas, plasterer
Elton Joseph, bricklayer
England Jos., plasterer and painter
Evans Sarah, ditto, ditto
Evans Thomas, ditto, ditto
Evans Thomas, ditto, ditto, Salford
Embleton John, painter
Farrell and Griffith, joiners
Fairweather John, plumber
Findlay Thos., plasterer and painter
Gresty James, joiner
Graham James, ditto
Garratt John, bricklayer
Gilmore Thomas, ditto
Gillespie Jos., plasterer and painter
Griffiths and Day, plumbers
Hay, Nish, and M'Kean, builders
Houston William, ditto
Heseltine Jeffrey, ditto

Hunt Charles, ditto
Harrison and Son, plumbers
Howard and Atkinson, ditto
Hurlbutt George, ditto
Heyworth and Lamb, ditto
Hayley and Collins, ditto
Hine and Shields, ditto
Heathcote William, ditto
Heyes George, ditto
Holland James, ditto
Harrison George, painter
Hodson Wm., plasterer and painter
Harper Humphrey, painter
Ireland John, joiner
Johnstone David, ditto
Jebson William, ditto
Jackson Robert, ditto
Judd George, bricklayer
Jones Thomas, ditto
Jones John, slater
Ker Andrew, builder
Kirkley George and John, slaters
Kay John, plasterer and painter
Kirkham William, ditto, ditto
Litherland James, joiner
Lamb Henry, ditto
Lewis John, bricklayer
Lamb Robert, ditto
Lloyd William, plumber
Livingtone James, ditto
Lowe John, slater ‖
Lomas Robert, plasterer and painter
Mellor and Greenhalgh, builders
M'Fee John, ditto
Moore and Greenshields, ditto
M'Lane Robert and James, ditto
Mellor William, ditto
Morley Thomas, bricklayer
Murray John, ditto
M'Cann William, painter
Metcalfe William, plumber
Norbury Francis, joiner
Owen John, ditto
Owen and Robinson, plumbers
Ogden Paul, ditto
Ogden John, slater
Pauling G. C. and Co., builders, &c.

Parry Richard, joiner
Russell Robert, ditto
Robinson William, ditto
Rowland William, bricklayer
Rowland David, ditto
Robinson Christopher, plumber
Ratchford Frederick, ditto
Rothwell Thos., plasterer and painter
Statham Isaac, builder
Stother and Richards, joiners
Sidebottom John, bricklayer
Sinclair William, plumber
Simmons Thos., plasterer and painter
Sandaver Richard, ditto, ditto
Smith Robert. ditto, ditto
Taylor and Williams, builders
Trees William, ditto
Trees Richard, Executors of, ditto
Turner John, builder
Turner W. and J., ditto
Tongue James, ditto
Tomlinson John, bricklayer
Tomlinson William, ditto
Turner John, plumber
Thyer Joseph, ditto
Townsend John, ditto
Thompson Joseph, ditto
Wilson Andrew, joiner
Watmough James, ditto
Witty William, ditto
Williamson James, ditto
Webster Thomas, ditto
Wood Joseph, ditto
Warburton Henry, ditto
Ward John, bricklayer
Williams John, ditto
Wilson ——, ditto
Wright William, ditto
Williams and Bradbury, ditto
Wright John, ditto
Winder John, plumber
Ward and Leach, ditto
Walters James, slater
Walters William, ditto
Wilkinson Thomas, ditto
Ward William, plasterer and painter
Young and Meikle, joiners

JOHN CAIRNS, Hon. Sec.

The following advertisement was also inserted by them in all the provincial papers:—

Wanted, in Manchester and the neighbourhood, about 4,000 workmen belonging to the following branches of the Building Trade, at the annexed rate of wages:—

Carpenters and Joiners 28s. per week for good workmen.			
Bricklayers .... 30s.	do.	do.	do.
Plumbers.................. 27s.	do.	do.	do.
Slaters .... 26s.	do.	do.	do.
Plasterers and Painters 26s.	do.	do.	do.
Labourers .... 18s.	do.	do.	do.

Apply (if by letter, prepaid) to Mr. John Cairns, Secretary, No. 1, Ducie Place, Exchange Buildings, Manchester.

The carpenters' and joiners' club then issued the following in answer to the address of the masters.—It will be seen in their subsequent address, that they were not authorized to make use of the names of the parties attached at the foot :—

TO THE PUBLIC.

We, the Operative Carpenters and Joiners of Manchester, Salford, and their vicinities, wish to rectify some unfounded statements which appeared in the *Guardian* paper on Wednesday last.

We beg to state, that we have not used any unjust interference, or dictatorial demands, more than the just request of wages, as before stated; yet we have been indiscriminately calumniated as the cause of compelling our employers to form themselves, in connection with all the other branches of the building trades, into a combined association to resist our demands. If such has been compulsory upon them, we, the operatives, have a just and legitimate right to state that we also were compelled. In 1843, when our union was near its dissolution, and without any exertion to renew it, our employers, finding our reluctance, took the advantage of reducing our wages 2s. per week. So fully were they determined, that some of them turned all their hands out of employ at once; then turning round upon them, stated, if they would accede to a reduction of 2s. per week from their wages, they might resume their work; others taking it week by week, indiscriminately, until they accomplished their end; while others complained of the unwarrantable proceeding, because they had not had a notice of it, but persisted in the reduction. So much was this the case, that many of the best workmen had not more than 25s. per week, and they averaged under 24s. 6d. By this method we were reduced, by those who exclaim they have no desire to reduce wages, and reprobate protection amongst the working class. Those heavy reductions, and threatened with more (the amount of which, we are afraid, did not go to the public), compelled us to renew our moral protection, and form ourselves into a protective body, which had, in some measure, the desired effect of advancing our remuneration in part, but not to the alleged standard. We deny any dictation, respecting either the amount of wages they give any individual, capacity, or number, or to compel men to join our society. This the employers must bear us out in, knowing that many have worked peaceably amongst us who did not belong to the society. We can also bear ourselves out from those intolerant transactions which are imputed to us, in causing any strike against a fellow-operative, or retarding the progress of work. These things becoming public, are attempted to be pressed upon you; but facts, which have been and are herein stated, will clear the understanding from prejudice against us, as much so as they have had the contrary operation upon those who have used so much calumny, the only weapon of defence they can resort to. If epithets such as these be their protection, we have no desire to shield ourselves under such; but leave our cause to a generous public, to determine betwixt us and those with whom we are contending for our pittance; and we hope to be able to keep ourselves in that respectability, for which we are so desirous and anxious to labour.

By Order of the Committee of Operative Carpenters
and Joiners in Manchester.

Carpenters' Hall, March 11th, 1846.

All persons desirous of completing the work they have in hand, in the carpenters' and joiners' department, may have the same finished substantially and with dispatch, by applying to the undermentioned employers, viz. :—

Messrs. Wm. and Henry Southern, Chapel-street, Salford
Mr. John Statham, Pendleton
Messrs. Bell and Worthington, Hulme
Mr. C. Woodburn, Todd-street
Mr. Jas. Dalton, Hulme-street, Salford
Mr. Clayton, Broughton
Mr. Leigh, Higher Temple-street, Chorlton
Mr. E. Birkett, Oldfield-lane, Salford
Mr. Clarke, Rusholme
Messrs. Tunstall and Draffin, Zara-street, Chorlton
Messrs. Moore and Son, Ancoats-street
Mr. T. Dent, Lower Mosley-street
Mr. Tweddell, near the Catholic Chapel, Hulme
Mr. Artingstall, Pendleton
Messrs. Eastwood and Tavo, Charles street, Chorlton
Messrs. Kitchen and Thompson, Chester-road
Mr. Smith, Greek-street, Chorlton
Mr. Redhead, Hulme
Mr. Younghusband, Portland-street
Mr. Warhurst, Pin Mill Brow
Mr. Knox, Saint Mary's
Mr. Samuel Ross, Gray-street
Mr. Storey, Salford
Mr. J. Wrench, Bloom-street, Salford
Mr. H. Kenyon, Regent-road.

Mr. John Webster, Charles-street, St. John's
Mr. Booth, Quay-street, Manchester
Mr. Stothard, Hulme
Messrs. Fitton and Ingleworth, Cheetham-hill
Mr. Robert Wood
Messrs. Parkinson and Penk, Red Bank
Mr. Robinson, Oxford-road, near Saint Peter's
Mr. Samuel Smith, Miles Platting
Mr. John Barton, Crown-street
Mr. Edward Slater, Liverpool-street
Mr. Barlow, Crown-street
Mr. Newby, Strangeways
Mr. J. Shuttleworth
Mr. Gresty, River-street, Hulme
Mr. R. Russell, Oldfield-road
Mr. John Bell, Alport Town
Mr. E. Taylor, Broughton
Mr. Turner, Grosvenor-square
Mr. R. Cant, Stretford New-road
Messrs. T. and P. Parry, Bennett-street
Mr. Charleton, Ardwick
Mr. Clayton, Cheetham-hill
Mr. D. Johnson, Angle-street, Chorlton
Mr. Drury, Stretford New-road
Mr. S. Cox, Lower Broughton
Mr. Hudson, Water-street
Mr. John Mason, Back Piccadilly
Mr. John Copeley, Salford
Mr. Nelsons, Greengate, Salford

Or at the Carpenter's Hall, where a number of good workmen may be obtained.—Carpenter's Hall, March 12th, 1846.

In the *Manchester Guardian*, of March 14th, an article of considerable length appeared, giving a general statement of the position of affairs between masters and men. It would exceed the reasonable limits which should be observed in such a work as this to insert the whole of the article. It was in the main correct; and certainly neither its errors nor its spirit were such as to justify the strong language which is used in the following reply to it :—

TO THE PUBLIC.

Th Carpenters and Joiners of Manchester having been attacked by an unfounded paragraph in the columns of the *Manchester Guardian*, feel it their duty to make the following public reply to the same :—

18

To the Editor of the Manchester Guardian.

Sir,—Your publication of Saturday last contains an article headed "The Joiners and Bricklayers's Strike," which, for gross falsehood and slander, stands unparalleled in our experience. As a large body of tradesmen, we have a right to demand of you, as a public journalist, the same means of rebutting those charges as you have afforded space for making them; but we do denounce emphatically the system pursued by you of publishing a party statement in favour of the employers, without enquiring on both sides of the question: for we are prepared with the most incontrovertible testimony to prove that the statements you have made are directly untrue. We deny, in the most unqualified terms, that we ever attempted to impose restrictions on our employers, either as to the mode of carrying on their business, or as to whom or who they should not employ; and you unhappily cite the case of Messrs. Pauling as an instance, a case which must be fresh in your memory. Mr. Pauling required every man in his employ to work 105 hours more every winter than any other master builder ever did: hence the dispute with Mr. Pauling,—and so much for your selection of an illustration of our present position. But it would seem that no stone should be unturned by you to place us in a false position with the public. We deny that we ever interfered with our employers as to the number of apprentices they should have. We deny that we ever extorted the reluctant consent of our employers to shorten the hours of labour; the time that we now work, taking the year round, is the same as it always has been. You, sir, state that the old hours were, during the winter, from six o'clock to six, and from the 17th of November to the 2nd of February, to light up and work until seven in the evening. This, sir, is directly untrue; and never was such a rule acted upon in Manchester. The working rule prior to last autumn was, from the 17th of November to the 2nd of February, to commence work at half-past seven in the morning, and leave off at seven in the evening; and from the 2nd of February to the 17th of November, to work from six o'clock to six, except Monday and Saturday, when we commenced at seven o'clock on the former, and left off at four o'clock on the latter. Now it must be obvious, that before the 17th of November, and immediately after the 2nd of February, there are several weeks we cannot see the whole time; this has been unpleasant alike to the employers and operatives, and also to the public. In order to allay this unpleasantness, we submitted to propositions to our employers,—the one to adopt the half-holiday, by commencing at six o'clock in the morning, and working until six in the evening, the year round, except Monday and Saturday, to commence at seven o'clock on the former, and leave off at twelve o'clock on the latter; the other by commencing at the same time and working until half-past five o'clock, and leaving work at four o'clock on Saturday afternoon. The former proposition was unanimously adopted by the whole of the master builders, with one exception, and was forthwith acted upon, each party considering they had neither gained nor lost by the alteration. This change took place in October last. Now mark the dishonourable attempt on the part of the employers to filch from us the half-holiday, which is due to us until October next, in consideration of the time we worked extra during last winter. We ask the public, is this fair and honourable dealing? Give us the half-holiday which is our due until next October, and we are then willing to re-consider the subject of time. All we require at our employers' hands is fair and honourable dealing. We deny distinctly that double time is charged by us after having worked two hours over time. Double time does not commence until after ten o'clock at night; and this was made for doing away with night labour. Your remarks respecting wages in London, Liverpool, and other towns, are also untrue; the wages in the two former being 2s. more than you have stated. After other remarks respecting a few individuals ruling and overawing the mass of the men, and other equally untrue statements, you assert that there are 1,700 men out of work. Here, again, sir, you stand convicted of falsehood. The numbers taken from the books was, last week, 1,002; and you further state they have to depend upon the miserable pittance of from 5s. 6d to 6s. per week. This, again, is untrue. Every man who answered his name for the first three days received 7s. 6d., the books being made up to Wednesday night, according to rule: and every man last week, on strike, received a full week's strike pay : so much for the state of our funds. In fact, the whole paragraph is, from beginning to end, line for line, a tissue of gross falsehood and calumny, published with the evident intention of prejudicing the public against a body of working men, endeavouring to raise themselves in the scale of society, without injury to any party. If a public journal be of any moral use, it ought to be the medium through which correct information should be conveyed to the public, especially in matters of dispute; and not, as in this case, the means of slandering and calumniating a body of workmen for the interest and gratification of their employers, calculated only to excite the worst passions of men, and widen the gap of friendly intercourse which ought to exist between the employer and operative; and which you, as a public journalist, ought to be the foremost to cultivate. In palliation of your statements, you may contend you have made them upon wrong information ; but it was your duty, as an editor, to have consulted both parties, and then you would have arrived at a more correct report. It may not be generally known what wages our employers pay; but we will set the public right upon this point. We take the seven principal employers, and in them we find 16 men receiving more than 26s. per week, 219 at 26s., 92 at 25s., 103 at 24s., and 152 receive less than 24s.; so that the public will see that our wages do not average more than 24s. 6d. per week. You taunt us with dictating to the men when they shall work, when they shall strike, what wages accept, and what offers refuse, which is altogether untrue, as there are more than 600 of our members at work. But can anything equal the tyranny of the master builders going to the small tradesmen, and threatening, if they did not turn their men out and join their union, they will withdraw the whole of their trade from them? Again, you state that the good workmen are mainly disposed to return to their work at the offer made. This again is untrue, for it is the best workmen who want rewarding for their talent. We also deny that we ever borrowed from, or stand indebted to, any trade in any town, as we have so far been able to pay our way. The whole of the charges we have denied, we are prepared to prove are untrue; and challenge either yourself or the masters' union, by deputation or otherwise, to meet before the Mayor, or any given number of arbitrators, and incontestibly prove they are directly and unqualifiedly false. And now, sir, for the whole matter in dispute. It was agreed last autumn that we should ask our employers for an advance of 6d. per day on our then rate of wages; and at the commencement of the present year, each employer was served with a formal notice to that effect,—the notice terminating on the 2nd of March : and we confidently appeal to the public whether our demand is unreasonable or not. Glance at the iron trades, and compare their wages with ours, without taking into account the amount of money it takes to furnish ourselves with tools, and a constant expense for the wear and tear of the same, that no other trade is subject to. This, then, is the whole of the dispute, unconnected with any other matter. It was this, and this alone, that caused Mr. D. Bellhouse to summon the masters together to form their present union; and the justness of our demand we shall leave to a generous and impartial public.—By order of the Committee.

We wish it to be understood, that the employers who are giving the wages, did not desire us to publish their names. We did it on our own account, merely to let the public know where they might have their work executed.

This reply called forth the following counter-statement on the part of the *Manchester Guardian,* on the 21st of March, which may be allowed to speak for itself:—

THE STRIKE IN THE BUILDING TRADES.
THE JOINERS AND CARPENTERS.

[The following article was prepared for publication on Wednesday, but excluded from want of room.]

In reference to the article which appeared in the *Guardian* of Saturday last, on the subject of the present strike in the building trades, we have been waited upon by a deputation of two carpenters and joiners, on behalf of their trade, with a written statement, alleging that the whole of our article is untrue from beginning to end; and they proceed then to specify various instances in which they assert its inaccuracy consists. We are desirous to do them the justice to publish these denials; and we therefore copy such parts of the substance of their statements, divested of the intemperate and improper language in which they were expressed, as appear to deny any fact or statement published in our last. They say—

"We deny, in the most unqualified terms, that we ever attempted to impose restrictions on our employers, either as to the mode of carrying on their business, or as to whom they should or should not employ."

We do not know whether the workmen attach the same meaning as ourselves to the term "restrictions on employers." Let us give an instance of what we mean: We are informed by an employer that a builder was erecting a warehouse in this town, and when some bricks were brought upon the ground the bricklayers and their labourers struck, on the ground that the bricks were "illegal;" and the joiners and carpenters also quitted their work, not because they had anything to complain of in their own trade, but merely to assist the bricklayers in imposing restrictions on the employers. The alleged illegality of the bricks having been removed, the building was proceeded with, when a second strike was made, on the ground that the master was employing an "illegal slater;" and on this occasion, not only did the slaters leave work, but they also caused the bricklayers and their labourers, the joiners and carpenters, and the plumbers to follow their example, and they made an attempt to compel the stonemasons to leave their work; but that trade having no connection with the general union of the building trades, refused to comply. These are what we call restrictions on employers. The next denial is as follows:—

"We deny that we ever extorted the reluctant consent of our employers to shorten the hours of labour."

We should perhaps have said, to redistribute the hours of labour. Several masters have declared to us, that an attempt made by two persons, neither of them principals, to obtain the half-holiday, met with the most decided opposition from the masters generally, and fell to the ground; and some time afterwards the workmen revived the proposition, canvassed the masters individually, and as they were all very busy at that time, they were desirous to avoid any strike, and a master, asked individually, answered to the effect, that if the other masters agreed to it, he would not oppose it; and in this way it was effected, without any written agreement on the part of the masters, and without their ever being called together on the subject. They state that their consent was reluctantly given. The next thing denied by the men is a matter arising out of a mere typographical error in our article of Saturday last, viz., that

"The old hours were from six to six during the *winter,* and, from the 17th November to the 2nd February, to light up and work till seven o'clock."

Now, it is clear from the context, that from November to February includes the winter, and that therefore the former part of the sentence refers not to the winter, but to the summer, and the word is italic should be summer. Since this article was prepared, the workmen have ordered the insertion of their statement, as an advertisement. It appeared on Wednesday; and for the statement of hours, and for all the statements of the men, we refer our readers to that advertisement. We are assured that the hours, between November and February, did not universally commence at half-past seven, but in many shops at seven o'clock. In other respects, the statement of the men, as to what we have called the old hours, appears to be correct. The men next say—

"We deny distinctly that double time is charged by us after having worked two hours over time. Double time does not commence till after ten o'clock at night."

On further inquiry, we learn that on this point we were mis-informed, and that double time commenced not at nine, but at ten o'clock. The men then state—

"Your remarks respecting wages in London, Liverpool, and other towns, are also untrue, the wages in the two former being 2s. more than you have stated."

Our statement was that in London

"The wages of carpenters and joiners do not average more than 28s. weekly. In Liverpool the wages in this trade are only 24s., or 4s. less than what the Manchester masters offer ; and we understand that the rate of their wages in Liverpool is usually 2s. a week lower than that of Manchester."

To this we may now add, that although, in London, clever, skilful hands (carpenters and joiners) command 30s., there are great numbers working for 26s., and we were told that the average of the whole was more likely to be 27s. than 28s. ; but we do not desire to overstate anything, and therefore took 28s. as the average, and now repeat the statement. At Liverpool, during the winter, the men do not light up at all, and their money wages are 2s. a week less than in Manchester. We are informed that the workmen, before the recent turn-out at Birkenhead, were receiving only 24s. a week ; they demanded 26s., and turned out to obtain it, and the masters have since agreed to give them 25s., at which price they have resumed work. The price offered by placard, by the Manchester employers, for good hands (carpenters and joiners), is 28s., or 3s. more than what the men have accepted at Birkenhead. The next allegation is, that our remarks respecting a few individuals ruling and overawing the mass of the men are untrue. We can only state what we are informed, that they compelled many who were not unionists to turn-out with them, and then refused to give them any support from the funds, unless they would join the union. Again, last Saturday evening, every carpenter and joiner at work in the town, as we are informed, had to pay a levy of 9s. 6d. on his week's wages, in support of the strike ; and we have heard of some men declaring that they would return to their work the next morning, but for the apprehension that they are under of assaults and ill-treatment from the unionist turn-outs, or, as they termed it, " having bricks thrown at their heads." One of these men emphatically declared, that he would rather work for 20s. a week than be humbugged as he was by the union, if he only knew how to proceed. The joiners next deny the truth of our statement, that the number of carpenters and joiners out of work is 1,700. We only professed to give the best enumeration we were able to obtain; and we are assured that the number who at first turned out was not far short of 1,700 ; but many have obtained work or left the town, or gone into machine shops and other places; while many who are not unionists are not counted by the men. The deputation repeatedly spoke of the very satisfactory information obtained from the workmen by the London reporters ; yet the *Times* estimated the number of joiners and carpenters alone out of work at 4,000. We are informed that one of the turn-outs stated that the number out last Friday was 1,187 ; this agrees with the estimate of the masters as to the probable number remaining, and is not very much higher than the statement of the deputation that "the number taken from the books [of the union, we suppose] last week, was 1,002." The deputation state that—

"It is untrue that the men have to depend on the miserable pittance of from 5s. 6d. to 6s. per week. Every man who answered his name for the first three days received 7s. 6d., the books being made up to Wednesday night, and every man last week received a full week's strike pay."

What that was, the deputation do not say. It seems the first payment to the turn-outs was for half a week, and not for a whole week; and in this respect, therefore, we were erroneously informed. The deputation deny that there is any dictation: we have mentioned some examples of what we call dictation; and on these the public must judge for themselves. They deny that the good workmen are mainly disposed to return to their work. We have reason to believe, from what we have heard, that there are many who are employed who are determined not to contribute such heavy levies as 9s. 6d. a week to the union; and many who have been induced to turn out, would return to work immediately, but for the apprehensions they entertain of the u: ion; for if the workmen eventually succeed in obtaining what they want, all who have quitted the body will be marked as "illegal men," with whom the others refuse to work. The men add—

"We also deny that we ever borrowed from, or stand indebted to, any trade in any town, as we have so far been able to pay our way."

The deputation called upon us twice on Monday morning, and again on Tuesday afternoon. The first time they said they had to see the sawyers to get from them a document, declaring our statement, as to two loans from the sawyers of £120. and £60., to be altogether untrue. On their last call they never produced any document, but their written statement contains the above denial. We can only add, that we are assured the sawyers themselves have made the statement, and that they will not deny it. In conclusion, the writers give their account of the origin of the present strike. On the other hand, the masters say they have not interfered with the men in any way; that they have held no meeting amongst themselves since 1833, till they were driven to form themselves into an association, last month, for mutual protection against the new demand of an advance of 3s. per week. All they desire, as they state, is a return to the old hours, averaging 57 or 57½ weekly the year round, instead of the new hours, which, with carpenters at out-door work, in many cases does not average more than 40 hours per week.

The following advertisement is interesting, as it exhibits the feeling which prevaded the general public mind :—

At a meeting of Architects held at the Queen's Hotel, March 18th, 1846, for the purpose of taking into consideration the serious inconvenience arising from the dispute now pending between the masters and their workmen connected with the building trade, and to take such measures as under the circumstances may be deemed necessary,

It was resolved unanimously—

"That, having considered all the matters connected with the present turn-out, as set forth in the statements published by the several parties, we think it our duty to advise our employers to suspend all building operations until the dispute be settled."

Richard Lane, chairman	Butterworth and Whittaker
Starkey and Cuffley	John E. Gregan
J. and J. P. Holden	Frank T. Bellhouse
Dickson and Brakspear	Edward Walters
Travis and Mangnall	E. H. Shelland
T. Fish Taylor	George Shorland.
Irwin and Chester	John Wolstencro
Alexander W. Mills	

Things had reached this position, when the masters, thinking that sufficient time had been allowed for the consideration of their offer of 2s. per week advance, determined to issue the following advertisement :

1, Ducie Place, Exchange Buildings, Manchester,
March 25th, 1846.

The Operative Carpenters and Joiners are informed, that in consequence of the offer of the Masters of the above trade of an advance of 2s. per week to the wages formerly paid not having been accepted by the Journeymen, the Central Committee of the Master Builders' Association have come to the resolution, that, if the terms are not accepted before the expiration of this week, the above offer will be withdrawn.

JOHN CAIRNS, Hon. Sec.

This advertisement was followed up by the publication of a placard, of which the following is a copy : —

At a general meeting of the Master Builders' Association, held at the Albion Hotel, Manchester, March 30th, 1846, the following resolutions were unanimously passed :—

1st.—That the proposal which has been made by this society to the turn-out Journeymen not having been acceded to, all communications between this Society and the General Trades' Union are at an end.

2nd.—That the Masters in the building trade, who are connected with this Society, will, in future, employ no Journeymen except such as are willing to sign a declaration that they do not belong to any General Trades' Union, and pledge themselves not to assist or subscribe to any Society which has for its object interference with the established rules of the trade.

3rd.—That this Society pledges itself to protect and encourage such work-men as are willing to accept employment on the above conditions.

JOHN CAIRNS, Hon. Sec.

This is the state of affairs at this moment as regards Manchester. The Union men are standing out, and the masters seem equally determined not to give way. Many of the workshops have received the full compliment of men who do not belong to the Union, and the others are daily becoming filled; but the Committee of the Union have managed, with great address, to get the men to deposit their tool-chests at the Carpenters' Hall, their head quarters, so as to prevent their acting independent of the body.

LIVERPOOL, BIRKENHEAD, & LANCASHIRE.

It would be but an imperfect discharge of the task I have undertaken if I did not call attention to the Building Trades elsewhere than in Manchester. I will do this very briefly. Since 1833, when the formidable combination of that year was effectually broken up, things went on comfortably on both sides. All bad feeling was forgotten, and from that period to within a week of the present time no meeting of masters for any purpose had taken place. In 1836, times being good, and work abundant, the Liverpool and Birkenhead masters advanced bricklayers, plasterers, masons, and joiners, from 24s. to 26s. per week during the summer months, the wages being 26s. from 1st March to 1st November, and 24s. from 1st November to 1st March. During the last year, however, the masters had great difficulty in getting a fair day's work done by many of the workmen. The labourers ceased carrying 14 bricks, and determined on carrying 12 only. Many of them refused to wheel materials in a barrow; and it became well known that a revival of the Trades' Union had taken place, and that any labourer was fined by the Union who carried the usual number of bricks, or wheeled them in a barrow. During the spring the men in all trades refused to commence work outside the boundaries of the town until half-past six in the morning, and they left off at half-past five in the afternoon. This was not opposed, and another move took place. They agreed that they would not commence work on the Monday morning until seven in the town, and half-past seven outside the town, and that they would leave off on the Saturday in the town at four o'clock, and outside at half-past three. This also the masters agreed to. Then came a resolution that they would not submit to any reduction during the winter quarter, but would have the same wages as in the summe . This also the masters submitted to. During the winter, which has been open and favourable, the masters have had so little done in proportion to the wages paid, that a constant irritation has been going on, and the demeanour of the great body of the men has been such, that it was evident something effectual must be done. From communications which were received, as well as from notices served, and from the meetings which were held by the workmen, all of which were summoned by placard, it became known that a strike was to take place; and although it was not publicly promulgated, it was clearly ascertained that an increase of wages and a diminution of the hours of labour were the objects aimed at. But having learned a lesson by the great strike in 1833, no *general* turn-out took place; but a strike occurred at Birkenhead, and 1,200 men, principally bricklayers, masons, and joiners, left their employment for an advance of wages. After a fortnight had elapsed, the Birkenhead masters discovered that the men on strike were receiving aid from those in Liverpool, and as it was clear that to attack *in detail* was the policy of the clubs, it became a question whether the masters at Birkenhead should be sacrificed only, that the clubs with accumulated resources might attack in detail the various employs in Liverpool. A remonstrance was agreed upon and published in the hope that it might have an effect upon the workmen at Birkenhead. It had a good effect upon the joiners, many of whom returned to their work; but the bricklayers, masons, and others, still remained out. At this period a temperate letter was addressed by Mr. S. Holme, who is well known to be the employer of many workmen, and that letter I am permitted to subjoin. The strike at Birkenhead still continuing, and it being evident that some decisive step must be taken, and it being well known that many workmen ob ected to the union, and that many had reluctantly joined it, it was thought advisable to require all men to sign a declaration that they would not join or remain members of the union, and that they would not contribute to its funds, or permit the appropriation of the funds of any of the benevolent societies to trade purposes. This proposition was demurred to, and nearly all the workmen left their employers. Many have, however, since agreed to the proposition, and in one establishment nearly 100 men have signed the declaration and resumed their work. In various trades the same thing has occurred, and the strike is therefore not as general as might have been supposed.

Annexed is Mr. Holmes's letter and the statement of the Liverpool and Birkenhead masters : —

TO THE WORKMEN IN THE EMPLOYMENT OF MESSRS. SAMUEL AND JAMES HOLME.

If I am to judge from the events of the last few days, and also from circumstances which have come to my knowledge, I must be led to the conclusion that we are again on the eve of a general turn-out ; and I have no

B

doubt that, if a strike takes place, it will be a struggle of no ordinary character and duration. The extent of our employ prevents a personal discussion with you all, and I therefore take this opportunity of offering to you a few remarks, which I hope you will receive in the same spirit of kindness with which they are intended by me.

I have always avowed, both publicly and privately (and as far as I have had the power, have acted upon the conviction), that the interests of employers and workmen are identical, and cannot be separated without injury to both. I look upon a large employ as a large family, over which the head should be the ruler; and he should take a deep interest in the moral, as well as physical welfare of every member, however humble that member may be. It is as much his privilege as it is his duty to advise and to succour all who may be connected with him, and to be the friend of all, in those depressions and calamities which are of such frequent occurrence. This may be done consistently with the preservation of that due subordination which is the essential ground-work of order, and which is absolutely necessary to ensure the good government and comfort of the whole.

I know that in such an employ as this there must be a diversity of opinion on the subject of strikes and that some men are anxious to have an increase of wages with an abridgment of the hours of labour; and that they join trade clubs, and assist in coercing those of their fellow-workmen who keep aloof from such combinations. Others there are who appreciate the advantage of constant employment, who have suffered from previous strikes, and are desirous of remaining at their occupation. Now to *all* I address these remarks; so that in case a turn-out takes place, and distress be the consequence of it, I shall stand clear to my conscience in having thrown out a friendly warning to those in whose welfare I take, as is my duty, the most lively interest.

Thirteen years ago a formidable and extended combination was the result of several years of unusual prosperity, and as many of you well remember, the workmen in the building trade throughout Lancashire and Cheshire stood out for eighteen weeks. The demands made on that occasion by the trade clubs were of such an absurd character, that if even the master tradesmen had been so besotted as to have yielded to them, the public at large would not have done so. The demand was, that no person whatever should be allowed to contract for a building or other work, but that all should be done by the permission of a central and acting committee of workmen (no doubt the leaders of the union); and this committee, in the plenitude of well paid but usurped authority, were to dictate the prices which each person was to pay and receive for the work so done. Could anything more absurd—nay, ridiculous—have entered into the brain of man? And yet, strange as it may now seem to you, a turn-out for such objects lasted eighteen weeks. Had the terms been submitted to, no man in his senses would have laid out a farthing in buildings *as an investment ;* nothing would have been done except from dire necessity; and two-thirds of all the building branches in Lancashire would in three months have been without a day's employment. Even when the combination was broken up, and the men returned to work, a large amount of capital had found other channels, many buildings previously contemplated were abondoned, and nearly the whole summer was lost. The year afterwards proved to be a year of commercial depression and financial difficulties. Work became scarce—a season of slackness arrived—many workmen had sold their furniture and tools to eke out a living for their families during the long strike; and I shall not soon forget the misery and wretchedness with which I was made acquainted during the succeeding winter. Many a man, who had thus foolishly lost the previous summer, was glad to avail himself of a loan of money to pay off debts previously contracted; and we assisted not a few to re-purchase even their beds, which they had pawned during the summer when walking about. When I state that that strike cost the workmen above forty-five thousand pounds, I am stating a sum below the actual amount; and it is within my own knowledge that many thousand pounds were invested in various ways, which would have been invested in building but for the ill-advised and most unfortunate strike. And who were the fomentors of it, and who the sufferers? I speak not of all; but I do know that some of the leaders on that occasion were men who had little pretension to the character either of sober men or skilful wor..men. I do also know that some of those who, previous to the strike, were not worth a farthing, were able, within a few weeks of its termination, to invest large sums of money; and it is notorious that one man paid above £300. (and he did pay it, too, in hard cash) for the good-will and fixtures of a flourishing establishment, which enabled him to bid good bye to his fellow workmen for the rest of his days. The sufferers were hundreds of steady and well-disposed men, good workmen, who were always sure of employment, and at first-rate wages; these men had been compelled, against their wishes, to join in the turn-out, and they were most shamefully and cruelly victimized. One thing struck me most forcibly in that turn-out. It was this. The placards which were posted upon the walls, and which purported to be the addresses of the various trades, were, in the majority of cases, copied from placards which had been posted upon the walls of Paris, previous to the reign of terror in the great French revolution. Draw what inference you like from this; but it is a fact, and if any of you dispute the fact, if you will look in Alison's History of Europe you will find whole paragraphs of them there recorded, as having been on the walls of Paris fifty years ago.

Wages are regulated by laws which cannot be permanently altered either by employers or workmen. They even fluctuate in different localities. If times be good and labour be in demand, high wages will always be paid; if times be bad and employment be scarce, labour becomes abundant, and it is difficult to maintain the previous rate. If the price of labour in any particular branch becomes greater than the community can afford to pay, capital, being of a moveable nature, can find other investments either at home or abroad; because no man will, knowingly, invest his money in that which will not yield him a fair and equitable return. If a house is to cost £1,200. where it ought only to cost £1,000., the house, in many cases, will not be built—a man can do better with his money. If wages rise beyond a certain level, which cannot be fixed either by masters or men, but which are regulated by financial matters—by commercial changes—by the produce of our soil, our looms, and a hundred other circumstances acting in unison; then they are like fluids which are forced up beyond their natural level, and both require an external force to keep them in their unnatural position. Withdraw the pressure, and they soon find their level.

It is a great mistake to suppose that a master tradesman profits by low wages, or suffers when wages are raised. *It is the public that pay the wages, and not the master tradesmen.* If higher wages than 26s. a week are now to be paid, it will, indeed, operate as a loss to us, so far as our present contracts are concerned; but only to that extent, because not only ourselves, but every body else must have increased prices for all future work. But, in such case, you may rest assured that the *public*, whom no club or Trades' Union can reach, will soon diminish the quantity of employment; and, instead of mechanical labour being at a premium, it will, in a short time, be at a discount.

We might, indeed, have a continual struggle with our workmen. The workmen taking advantage of the summer to demand an increase—the masters retaliating in the winter by making a reduction; and so both parties would live in perpetual turmoil, and waste their lives in useless contests, where, in effect, both parties would be losers. But would such a state of things be desirable? Would not exasperated and bitter feelings be the result? Would not animosity and suspicion be engendered, which would destroy all comfort in business, and which would be contrary to that Christian spirit which ought to actuate every man, rich or poor, in his dealings with his fellow-man? I cannot conceive any thing more destructive than such struggles; and he can be no friend to the happiness of the working classes, who attempts to create such fueds between them and their employers. No respectable contractor, possessing capital, would, under such circumstances, run the risk of taking work which might last two or three years. He would not afford that accommodation to many persons which they need, and without which accommodation many buildings would not be erected. He would cease to make provision for the employment of his workmen during the w nter season (and which builders often do at great loss to themselves), because he would have no inducement to help through a winter those men who, on the first approach of spring, would be arrayed in hostility against him. Such, however, have been, and, I fear, will again be, the results of workmen yielding a blind acquiescence to the commands of a trade club, the members, or rather the committee of which, feeling no want, are dead no sympathy; and having no responsibility, naturally arrive at a state of tyrannical dictation.

In making these remarks, however, I admit that workmen have a perfect right to combine, and that an association may, in many respects, be made advantageous, if properly conducted. The working man has a perfect right to sell his labour at the highest price he can get, because it is his capital; but when a combination is misdirected—when every employer, however considerate and benevolent, is denounced in a club-room as a tyrant and oppresser—when violent language is used, and bitter feelings are engendered, between those who ought to be the best friends—when every workman is ordered by a well-fed and well paid-directory to submit to their dictation, and to walk about for weeks together, whether he chooses or not—then, I think, the charge of tyranny ought to be transferred to those who are exercising a power which the Queen of England dare not, and ought not to exercise. To prevent any man labouring for whom, and on what terms he chooses, is a stretch of authority more consonant with the arbitary power exercised in Russia, than it is consonant with that freedom in England on which we so justly pride ourselves.

Then, again. A combination of masters can never take place, unless it is created by a combination of workmen whose demands are unreasonable. Last summer you requested that the working time on Mondays and Saturdays might, on each of those days, be abridged an hour. This was acceded to, although the concession costs us, small as it may seem to you, £600. a-year. The bricklayers then demanded 26s. a week during the winter months. This was also acceded to; but no combination of masters took place. It is now, however, quite clear that further demands are contemplated, and now the masters are driven, in self-defence, to meet for mutual support and protection for the first time these thirteen years, because the limit of reason is discarded, and it is apparent that a determined stand must now be made.

Now, I never yet knew a club satisfied. The importance of the officers is magnified during a strike—and it is in human nature to be deemed of importance. If workmen would only invest in the Savings' Bank the amounts paid into the coffers of the trades' clubs, many of them would, in a few years, be independent, not only of clubs, but of masters also. A good and steady workman is always valuable and sure of employment at good wages; but the idle or unskilful man feels the necessity of seeking that support from a combination which he cannot obtain by his own character and industry. Yet, the object of the clubs has, so far, been to reduce all men to the same level; and, on such an unjust system, the industrious—the skilful and the sober are made to contribute to the support of the idle—the dissolute—the unskilful. There are many men in this employ who are better worth 30s. a week than others are worth 20s., yet, amongst the bricklayers, and in the majority of the cases amongst the joiners, all are

29

paid alike; so that the character and ability go for nothing, but are merged into the unnatural levelling of the whole. Is this either just or reasonable? I state, with much sorrow, but truth and experience oblige me to state it, that an *increase of wages has always been followed by a diminution of labour*, also by a diminution of the number of hours per week worked by the aggregate number of men employed, and that we have no inducement in the prospect before us to expect otherwise than a still further diminution if wages were again advanced. This ought not to be the case, and some of you may be disposed to doubt it. Let me then prove it. Before the year 1834, when 24s. per week to bricklayers was regularly paid, our brick work cost us, in workmanship, sixpence per square yard on the average of three years' work. The wages were subsequently raised to 26s., and supposing an equal quantity of work to have been done, the workmanship ought to have cost us sixpence halfpenny, or one-twelfth more than it had previously done. Taking the years 1842, 1843, and 1844, we find it has cost us above eightpence halfpenny per yard, or 30 per cent. more than it did before the advance; and that in 1845 the cost has exceeded ninepence.

I adopt as sincerely as any of you the motto, "A fair day's wages for a fair day's work," and I will always pay the one and look for the other; for I should not be doing justice either to you or to our employers if I did not pay you well, and at the same time did not ask you to give the value of it in a fair and honest day's work. The duties are reciprocal, but the reciprocity is too often forgotten. My notion may be old-fashioned, but it is this. If 4s. 4d. a day be honestly paid, 4s. 4d. should be honestly earned; and the man who takes off the pay-table 26s. a week, when he has only given for it 20s. worth of work, infringes the principle of honesty as much as the man who unlawfully appropriates that which does not belong to him. On this point, however, I shall not say more.

I have had some experience as a practical workman, and know what it is to do a day's work as well as any man, and I do mean to assert, from having done it many a time, that thirty per cent. more work might have been done by the aggregate bricklayers during the last four years, and, taking the average, no man could be said to have done more than a fair day's work. How, then, can employers consent to a further advance under such circumstances? I could, if I was disposed, say much about the composition of the clubs which dictate to so many of you. Two facts only will I mention. The chairman of a recent trades' meeting was discharged from this employ because he was found asleep at three o'clock one fine afternoon, when making some repairs for a widow lady. He had closed the bed-room door and composed himself to sleep, and, had he not been discovered, would unquestionably have charged his full time. He is a good talker but a bad worker.

In 1833 I was one of a deputation to meet a number of the leaders of the Union, to endeavour to make some satisfactory arrangements, and prevent a turn-out. About sixty or eighty men were present. I looked round the room to see if I could discover any of our best and most valued workmen, but I looked in vain. The majority of those whom I knew, were men who never remained long in any employ; and the chief orator of the evening was a bricklayer, notorious for his indolence and inattention as a workman, (and in all sincerity I say it), who was not then, or ever was, before or since, worth employing at 2s. a day. I do not mean to say that all clubs are managed by such men. Far otherwise. Many men are misled in joining them, and many join them from good motives. But I do mean to assert that trade clubs have invariably done more mischief than good; and that they have levied contributions on thousands of workmen, for which they have given them no equivalent, except that of reducing many an honest man to want and misery, by embroiling him in unprofitable, and, in the majority of cases, useless strikes. I will suppose, however, that, by the coercion and influence of the clubs, an advance of 2s. per week could be

B 3

obtained. How long would it last? Just as long as there is a busy time, but no longer; for an advance of wages cannot be permanent in this locality, unless the people of Liverpool (yourselves among the number) are prepared to pay higher rents for their houses. A turn-out for one month will cause you, if successful, to work a whole year at the advanced rate to make up even that loss of time; but if unsuccessful, which I think will be the case, a turn-out of a month is equal to a reduction of 2s. per week for twelve months, making the wages for a year 24s. instead of 26s.

There is one class of workmen for whom I have always felt more sympathy than for others—it is our labourers, but more particularly the hod carriers. Their work is hard; they are exposed to the weather, and in winter they often lose much time; and yet, I am sorry to say, they are more misled than any other class of men, because their employment is that of mere physical force, which can be done much cheaper by machinery of the simplest and most portable description. In no country, except Great Britain, are hod carriers generally employed. I never saw one in any part of the continent; and it is not only more convenient, but more economical, in almost every instance, to *hoist* up materials, or use a wheelbarrow, than to pay men for *carrying* heavy loads up a ladder. We no more need to have bricks carried on men's shoulders than the merchant in hoisting his goods into a warehouse need adopt such an antiquated principle; yet I should be sorry to introduce machinery for this purpose, in every instance, as it would throw many poor men out of employment; but the labourers must be prepared for it, for the period is fast arriving when we shall be driven to hoisting instead of carrying, and a turn out of hod carriers will precipitate the measure.

I will not conceal from you my opinion that the present demand for mechanical labour will not be of long duration. A period of great prosperity has ever been followed by one of depression; and the extent to which speculation has been carried—the quantity of materials manufactured, the investment of borrowed capital, and the liabilities entered into by thousands who have no means of meeting them if a slight reverse takes place—these, and other circumstances, must put a stop to inordinate speculation—must make money more valuable—bankers more than usually cautious; and we must undergo a year or two of what is called "slack times" to bring us back to something like moderation. Now, I believe I am correct in saying that many of our merchants are, at this time, suffering much from a fall in prices, and from a variety of difficulties. I hear of no new and extensive undertakings about being entered into; and of those projected last year, many will never be executed, and for many others the money will not be found.

Extensive rows of houses have recently been built in this town and neighbourhood which are not wanted, and numbers of them are to be let; and, knowing much more about the way in which many of these houses are "got up" than you can know, you will find in a very short time, that dozens of them will have to be sold, because they are mortgaged most deeply, and interest of money never sleeps. This event, which is not far distant, will have the salutary effect of stopping, for a time, the erection of buildings which are not wanted. I do believe that a suspension of all buildings of every description for three months would be at this time, a great public convenience, and would tend to bring us back to a healthy system. There is not a public building, at this time, which needs to be hurried, and which may not stand still to advantage; and I know that many works, of various sorts, *would* stand still at this moment if there was the slightest cause or excuse for their being stopped. But the prospect is appalling, when we reflect upon the number of wives and children who would, of necessity, be involved in the calamity of such a stoppage of labour, and, consequently, of wages.

Let me not, however, be misunderstood. Do not suppose that I desire to inculcate the principle of passive obedience to anything that is wrong, or in the slightest degree oppressive. Do not suppose that I am an advocate for a man remaining a journeyman all his days. Many must of necessity do so; but I should rejoice to see all our younger men strike out a new path for themselves, and commence to do business on their own account. Every large concern has had a small beginning: and there is no law in England to keep a man a journeyman all his days. Industry, frugality, patience, and integrity,—these are the only solid foundations of future and permanent success. Let any man adopt these four words for his motto, and I prophesy that he will not long continue to be a labouring mechanic.

Nothing affords me greater pleasure than to see our young men rising into master tradesmen, and nothing is more gratifying than assisting them in their praiseworthy efforts. If any employer oppresses a man—refuses to pay him the full value of his labour—keeps him without his wages till a late hour on Saturday—pays him a farthing short of his due,—or pays him in a public house, or in anything but the lawful coin of the realm,—such an employer will have no sympathy from me, if workmen demur in these things. Man is a reasoning being: and the humblest labourer has a right to look for good treatment and civility from those who employ him; and well would it be for all classes if a better understanding existed amongst them,—if the workman was more subordinate, and the employer, in many cases, more considerate. I speak the sentiments of my brother as well as myself, when I say that it is our wish to see all our workmen well paid, their families comfortable, and themselves contented. We have spared neither pains nor expense to make them so, and have on many occasions incurred serious losses to keep together our usual establishment of workmen, and help them over a winter.

Trade clubs have neither feeling nor sympathy. On the contrary, they destroy both, and, while they point out an employer as an oppressor, they lay prostrate the independence of every workman; they subjugate his will; domineer over his person, chain him in mental slavery; and amidst the light and liberty of the 19th century, they neither allow a man to think nor act as he pleases. It is ridiculous for us to talk of "free-trade" while such monopolies are tolerated. A trade club is a monopoly of the most mischievous description when it operates by coercion, actual or implied.

Judge now for yourselves. Much shall I regret it if, on a calm and dispassionate consideration of what I have said, you still resolve to have a strike, I warn you that in the present uncertain state of the money market, and of our commercial relations, that it will do you no good, and you must not blame me, if, after some months, you are obliged to resume work at the old wages, when work is diminished and capital has been directed into other channels, and when you have been foolish enough to starve your families and yourselves upon 8s. or 10s. a-week of club allowance, instead of availing yourselves of the abundant employment which, as yet, the prosperous season has left for us, but which in twelve months may not be so abundant.

Believe me to be your sincere friend,

Benson-street, March 11, 1846. SAMUEL HOLME.

I am sure that no one can read the foregoing beautiful letter without feeling that it is a cheering sign for the days in which we live, to find a gentleman who has control over so large a body of operatives, and who possesses so great an influence from his station and worth, so fully alive to the mutual relations which should exist between master and men. Subjoined are the proceedings of two meetings held in Liverpool. These documents require no lengthened comment:—

At a Meeting of the Master Tradesmen of Liverpool and Birkenhead, engaged in the various departments of Building, and held the 10th March, 1846, at the Grecian Hotel, Dale-street, and where thirty-five of the most extensive firms were represented,

Mr. JOHN TOMKINSON in the Chair,

It was intimated that the Joiners and Masons of Birkenhead had struck work for an advance of Wages, and that most of the buildings at that place were suspended; and it appearing from notices recently served upon the Master Masons of Liverpool, as well as from other circumstances, that the strike at Birkenhead is only preparatory to a similar strike in this town,

It was resolved unanimously,—

1. That this Meeting, disavowing any intention of interfering with the wages or privileges of the workmen engaged in the building trade; and being desirous of maintaining that good understanding which ought to exist between employers and workmen, views with regret the steps that have been taken by some of the trades in their attempts to disturb existing and satisfactory arrangements.

2. That the present hours of labour are fair and reasonable—that the wages now paid by every respectable employer are as high as can be afforded, and this Meeting pledges itself to resist any attempt that may be made, either to raise the present rate of wages or to abridge the hours of labour.

3. That this Meeting feels unwilling to recommend the formation of an Association of Master Tradesmen, even for defensive purposes, although they may be compelled to do so by the unreasonable demands, not so much of the workmen themselves, as of the Trade Clubs; but while the individuals composing the present Meeting may regret the necessity, they are prepared unanimously to form such an Association, if the emergency of the case require it.

Signed on behalf of the Meeting,

JOHN TOMKINSON, Chairman.

––––––

At a Meeting of the Master Tradesmen of Liverpool and Birkenhead, which was held at the Grecian Hotel, Dale-street, on Monday last, the 23rd instant, and where sixty-one persons were present, representing forty-nine firms, engaged in the various departments of the Building Trades,

Mr. JOHN TOMKINSON in the Chair,

It was intimated that the strike at Birkenhead still continued, and that (excepting the joiners, who had resumed their employment), there was not at present any appearance of its termination; and from documents which were read, and from information which was given, it appearing that the turn-out is caused by the interference, and under the dictation, of the trades' unions, and that many of the workmen now engaged in Liverpool are contributing to the support of those who are standing out; and it being clearly ascertained that many workmen are dissatisfied with the proceedings of the clubs, and would willingly abandon them,

*It was unanimously resolved,—*That each of the masters now present will require every workman in his employment to sign a declaration that he does not, and will not, belong to, nor subscribe to, the funds of any trades' union, and will discountenance any appropriation of the funds of any sick or benefit society to the support of a turn-out of their own or other trades. And each employer now present (testified by his signature to this resolution) hereby declares that he will not employ any workman who refuses to sign such a declaration. JOHN TOMKINSON, Chairman.

The master tradesmen engaged in the various branches of building, in making public the foregoing resolutions, desire to record their regret that circumstances have rendered them so painfully necessary. Their object is not to reduce the wages paid to their workmen, not to increase the hours of labour, nor to revoke the concessions which they made the last year. They desire not to abridge the privileges or comforts of the workmen; but the baneful influence which is at present exercised by the secret and irresponsible tribunals of the trades' unions, so repulsive and unjust in all their tendencies, have rendered it imperative upon the employers to adopt the resolutions alluded to, not only in self-defence against the dictations of the unions, but for the purpose of shielding as much as possible the well-disposed, and, in almost every instance, the most valued of the workmen, from the tyrannical dictation of these dangerous combinations. So long as these combinations are permitted to interfere with the freedom which is the inalienable right of every man, whether he be an employer or an operative; so long as they are permitted to levy contributions upon every man, even against his will; so long as they promote discord, and cause uncertainty to rest upon every transaction, there is no security for any man in taking a contract, nor is there the most remote hope for a return to a better state of things, unless these unions, so contrary to the spirit of the times, and so repugnant to every principle, both of justice and humanity, are completely broken up or rendered powerless.

They hold that justice to the public, as well as to the operatives, requires that LABOUR, as well as CAPITAL, SHALL BE FREE; that every man ought to be at perfect liberty to dispose of his labour, which is his capital, when, where, and as he pleases; that it cannot be for the advantage of the working classes themselves, that a dictatorial inquisition should be established, and that an irresponsible agency should exist, to create a monopoly, and tax the industry of the many for the benefit of the few, who themselves in general are amply supported, and maintained out of the earnings of the well-disposed and the industrious. They assert that all restriction and prohibitions upon labour, all dictation to an employer *who* he shall employ, what wages he is to pay, and how his business is to be conducted, are the establishment of a monopoly of the most mischievous description, and which ought to be resisted by every man who values his personal liberty, and who claims for himself that freedom of thought and action which is the undoubted birthright of every man in England, be he rich or poor.

The trades' unions levy contributions, order or suspend strikes, and endeavour, as far as they have the power, to prevent any man disposing of his labour, unless he first enrols himself a member of the union, submits to its decrees, and contributes to its funds. They interfere with that freedom of trade which is so essential to the comfort as well as to the success of all building operations; and, at this time, great numbers of men are walking about in idleness at Birkenhead, Manchester, and other places—many of them most unwillingly—while there is abundant employment for them at 26s. per week, which is an advance of 2s. per week upon the wages paid during the period of the war, and until the year 1836, when a rise from 24s. to 26s. was cheerfully acceded to.

These men are not permitted to work, and hundreds of others are taxed to keep them in idleness. And it is well known that the workmen in Liverpool are directed to continue at their employment, and contribute a portion of their earnings to these at Birkenhead, who, if they should prove to be successful, will be required to contribute to the support of those in Liverpool, when a strike occurs in this town.

The master tradesmen most cheerfully recognise the principle, that labour should be paid for at the highest price which can be obtained for it; and they believe that the wages paid now are fully as high as the public can afford to pay; for it is the public, and not the master tradesmen, who have eventually to pay the wages. So far as they are concerned, it is not their interest to pay low wages; and all that they contend for is, the liberty of employing workmen at such wages as may be mutually agreed upon, without the unnecessary interference of a club, perhaps composed of men who do not even belong to the town, and whose interference is as mischievous as it is uncalled for.

To such dictation and interference they are firmly resolved not to submit, be the consequences what they may.

To meet the difficulties connected with the present strike at Birkenhead, they have the choice of two alternatives. One is, to suspend all work in Liverpool while that strike lasts; the other is, to require every workman to sign a declaration that he is not, and will not remain, a member of these dangerous combinations, which have been the bane of every community where they have been established. The former mode would be unjust towards those of their workmen who are not members of the union (and they rejoice to know that there are many such), and they have therefore adopted the latter alternative, because it will give to every man a free choice, and afford him an opportunity of quitting the trades' unions altogether.

They would fain hope that the majority of the workmen will accede to the proposition : but if it unfortunately happens that they should be disappointed in their hope, they confidently appeal to the public for that forbearance which it will be their duty to ask ; and they have already had assurances from many quarters, that the erection of buildings may be suspended until the workmen, as well as the masters, are relieved from the thraldom of such tyrannical combination.

John Tomkinson	Samuel & James Holme
John Johnson	Leader & Dooley
Furness and Kilpin	W. Troutbeck & Son
Joseph Boumphrey	John Bromley
Thomas Mackarel	James Crellin
Thomas James	Isaac Henshaw
Knight and Nimmo	James Stringfellow
James Gore	Richard Gardner
H. Haydock & Son	Thomas Tapley
Robert McKee	Edward Williams
Dempster & Wilson	John & James Lyon
Richard & Paul Barker	William Tomkinson
William Bateman	John Critchley
Thomas Gore	Thomas Jones
Richard Edwards	John Fulford
Owen Ellis	William Jones
John Morris	William Baker
George Robinson	Thomas Hughes
John Williams	James Holt
Alexander White	Thomas Wylie
Thomas Haigh	

J. & W. Walker, Birkenhead	William Jackson, Tranmere
Henry Gole, Ditto	James Hume, Birkenhead
James Routledge, Ditto	John Williams, Ditto
John Hogarth, Rock Ferry	John Hitchen, Ditto
William Oberry, Birkenhead	Joseph Wilkinson, Ditto
James Stephenson, Tranmere	Wemyss & Cameron, Ditto
Hugh Williams, Birkenhead	Joseph Leay, Rock Ferry
Job Richards, Ditto	S. Bailiff, Birkenhead

Upon being required to sign the declaration of disconnection with the union, the great majority of the workmen, quitted their employment; and a very excited state of feeling exists in Liverpool at the present moment.

APPENDIX.

Since the commencement of this compilation, several very important documents have been forwarded for our use, which might, perhaps, have come better in some previous portion of this Pamphlet, had they arrived earlier. As they will be of great use in the illustration of the matter in hand, and be alluded to in my subsequent remarks, they are here inserted :—

I.

TO THE VARIOUS BRANCHES OF THE BUILDING TRADE.

Fellow-workmen,—We, the United Branches of the Building Trades of Manchester, having agreed that the Plumbers and Glaziers of Manchester should " strike for an advance of wages;" and a great majority of the employers having agreed to give the said advance, a mere few of the would-be-tyrants. that exist in every town, have determined not to give this advance, and have held a meeting, and passed a resolution, that they should advertise for men in the surrounding towns.

We therefore give you notice to beware of such advertisement or any other attempt to delude strangers, by promising them things that they cannot perform. From this we entreat your kind assistance in preventing as much as possible the efforts of these petty tyrants.—We remain, yours,

THE UNITED BUILDING TRADES OF MANCHESTER.
October 2nd, 1845.

II.

Working Rules to be observed by the Carpenters and Joiners of Manchester, Salford, and their Vicinities.

That the working hours of the Carpenters and Joiners, in Manchester and Salford, be from Seven o'Clock on Monday morning until Six in the evening ; and from Six to Six all other days, except Saturday, on which day they cease work at Twelve at noon, making a total of 57 hours per week, Christmas and New Year's Eve excepted, on which days they cease work at dark.

That all men working out of doors in the winter season, shall work from daylight to dark; and from the 17th of November to the 2nd of February, shall take their breakfast before they commence working. All work done before and after the usual hours shall be accounted over-time, at the rate of two hours for a quarter of a day, until Ten o'Clock, and on Saturdays until Eight o'Clock ; after that time to be double time. Any man missing his time in a morning, quarter time will be ten minutes to Nine, and on Mondays half-past Nine ; but we wish to suggest to our employers the propriety of allowing them in such cases to commence at Seven o'Clock.

That all work done more than three miles from Manchester, lodging money of two shillings per week shall be allowed, and time to return on Saturdays to be at the shop by half-past Twelve o'clock, calculating to walk at the rate of three miles per hour, and the same allowance for Mondays as at the shop. All work done under three miles and more than half a mile from the shop, to have ten minutes allowed for every half mile above the latter distance No man will be allowed to work in buildings by candle light, when the same is not closed in, and made so that men may work without danger.

Should any man have occasion at any meal time, or morning, to go to his shop for timber, nails, &c., or on any business connected with his work, he must be there at the regular time to commence work, and shall be paid for his time however long he may be detained; and no piece-work will be allowed in any shop, neither shall we work with those that do.

By order of the Committee.

III.

RULES AND REGULATIONS

OF THE

ASSOCIATION OF UNITED TRADES FOR THE PROTECTION OF INDUSTRY.

OFFICE, 30, HYDE-STREET, BLOOMSBURY.

LONDON: PRINTED BY ORDER OF THE DELEGATES.

This Association is based upon two "great facts,"—first, that the industrious classes do not receive "a fair day's wages for a fair day's labour;" secondly, that for some years past their endeavours to obtain this have, with few exceptions, been unsuccessful.

The main causes of this state of things are to be found in the isolation of the different sections of working men, and the absence of a generally recognised and admitted authority, emanating from and supported by the Trades themselves, capable of exercising a centralising and controlling power over the movements of the labouring classes in cases of trades' difficulties, where nothing less than a national unity of action could place them in a condition either to withstand the encroachments on, or demand the rights of labour. It is therefore anticipated that by this organization each trade will multiply its powers, fifty or a hundred fold, by being enabled to fight its individual battle with the whole strength of the association.

While aiming at these important objects, it is at the same time no part of the objects of this Association to interfere with the existing Trades' Unions, but that the General Association of Trades should rather be grafted upon, and grow out of, these Unions, than supersede them. The peculiar local internal and technical circumstances of each particular trade, render it necessary that for all purposes of efficient internal government, its affairs should be administered by persons possessing a practical knowledge of them, and identified by personal interest and position with those for whom they act.

For these reasons, it is not intended to interfere with the organization of existing Trades' Unions, so far as they have reference to internal management and regulations; but simply to form a common centre, towards which their associated means may converge for mutual assistance and support in case of need.

GOVERNMENT.

Constitution.—The Association shall consist of those Trades' Unions and other organised bodies of the working classes that subscribe to its funds and conform to its laws, and have a stated time and place of meeting.

Conference.—The legislative power shall be vested in an annual Conference of delegates from the several Trades' Unions and other organised bodies in the Association.

Scale of Representation.—Trades' Unions and other organised bodies having not less than 30 nor more than 150 paying members may return one delegate. Trades with 150 and not more than 300 members, two delegates ; and one additional delegate for every 300 members above that number. All delegates shall be payable members of one of the societies they represent.

Unions of Organised Bodies for Representation.—In cases where the number of an organised body is less than 150, they shall be at liberty to unite with another organised body or bodies of the Association similarly situated, for the purpose of sending a delegate or delegates.

Annual Sessions.—An annual Session of Conference shall be held on Whit-Monday, in such town and place as may be determined upon by the Conference or Central Committee, and such conference shall continue its sittings so long as is requisite for the transaction of the business brought before it.

Special Sesssions.—The Central Committee shall have the power of convening a special session of Conference when it shall appear to a majority of at least three-fourths of the Committee that such a session is necessary, or upon a requisition of at least one-third of the members of Conference. In case the Central Committee neglect to call such special meeting on such requisition, the requisitionists shall have power to call it themselves. Not less than fourteen days' notice of all such special meetings shall be given to the delegates.

Business Paper.—One month previous to the assembly of the annual Conference, the Central Committee shall cause to be prepared and issued a business paper, or programme of the matters intended to be brought under the consideration of the Conference. Such programme shall be laid before the various trades, to enable them to give instructions to their delegates thereupon. But the Central Committee shall have the power of introducing subjects not included in the said paper, if agreed upon by three-fourths of the Committee, and such as appear to require the immediate attention of the Conference. Notices of special sessions shall include the business for which they are called.

Duties of Conference.—The Conference shall have power to make and revise the laws of the Association, subject to the following regulations :— No fundamental or important law shall be repealed or altered, without at least six months' notice having been given of such intended repeal or alteration, and concurred in by at least two-thirds of the Conference. Similar notice shall be given of all intended additions to the laws, and such additions be similarly approved of. To elect the Central Committee, to fix the salaries of the officers of the Association, and generally to transact all such business as may come before it.

Ex-officio Members.—Members of the Central Committee may sit and speak in Conference, though not elected as delegates, but in such case they shall not vote.

Tenure of Office.—The Delegates shall be elected to serve in Conference for twelve months, or until the next general election.

Elections.—Within one month previous to Whit-Monday, in each year, the Central Committee shall issue their precept to those trades and associated bodies entitled to send Delegates, requiring them to proceed, within fourteen days after the receipt of the same, to the election of a delegate or delegates to represent them in Conference for the ensuing year. And such precept shall be signed by the President and Secretary of the Association.

Nomination of Candidates for Central Committee.—At the meeting held by each associated body for the election of delegates to Conference, it shall be in the power of the members to nominate a list of persons as candidates for the office of Central Committee, such nominations to be communicated to the general secretary, who shall make out a list of all such nominations, and transmit it to the elected delegates one week before the day of meeting of conference.

Returns.—Each of the said trades and associated bodies shall, seven days previous to Whit-Monday, cause a return to be forwarded to the office of the Central Committee, certifying the delegate or delegates elected to represent such associated body, and such return shall be signed by the chairman of the meeting at which such election was made, and by the Secretary of the associated body.

Removals.—If any delegate, by absence or other cause, should become, in the opinion of the trade, or associated body, unfit to continue its representative, the said trade may declare the office vacant.

Vacancies.—On the death, resignation, or removal by the trade, of any delegate, the president and secretary of the trade by which such delegate was elected shall certify the same to the Central Committee, which shall forthwith issue their precept for the election of another to supply the vacancy.

Votes of Officers.—No salaried officer of the Association elected as delegate to Conference by any trade shall vote on questions personally affecting himself.

CENTRAL COMMITTEE.

Appointment.—The general executive power shall be vested in a Central Committee to be chosen annually by Conference.

Officers.—This Committee shall consist of a President, Vice-President, and eleven other members. The President and Vice-President shall be elected by the conference, without reference to their connexion with this Association, but the eleven other members shall be *bona fide* members of a trade society.

Qualification.—Five members of the committee shall be elected from the London trades, and six from the Provincial trades—the five members stationed in London to carry out the routine business of the Association, the remaining six to deliver their opinions and advice in writing, if necessary, except in cases of importance and difficulty, when they shall attend in person in London to superintend the business of the Association. The President and Vice-President shall belong to the London district.

General Secretary.—The General Secretary shall be elected at the Annual Conference, and shall hold his office so long as he performs his duties to the satisfaction of the Committee. And whenever the office shall become vacant, the Central Committee shall have the power to elect another Secretary, who shall hold office until the next Conference.

Treasurer.—The Treasurer to be elected and to hold office on the same terms as the Secretary.

Security from Officers.—The Treasurer and General Secretary shall give such security for the monies they may be entrusted with as the Central Committee may require.

Powers and Duties.—The Central Committee shall direct and control the general proceedings of the Association for and in the name of the Association. They shall receive all applications from the Trades for advice and assistance, and shall act thereon as they may deem requisite. They shall by mediation, arbitration, and legal proceedings, protect the interests and promote the well-being of the Associated Trades in all cases of trade disputes and difficulties. They shall promote all measures, political, social, or educational, which are intended to improve the condition of the labouring classes. They shall appoint such clerks, agents, and subordinate officers, as they may deem expedient. They shall summon the annual or special Conference, as provided by the laws; and, generally, they shall take the most efficient means in their power to promote the objects of the Association. In case of death or resignation of any member of the Central Committee the committee shall elect another of the conference delegates to fill the vacancy.

Levies.—The Central Committee shall be empowered to call for any levies from the associated trades as may be requisite for the maintenance of such measures for the protection of industry to which they may give their sanction. Any trade failing to remit such levies, without showing sufficient cause, shall forfeit all claim to the assistance of the Association. Such trades to have the right of appeal to the next Conference.

Quorum.—Five members of the Central Committee shall constitute a quorum, to transact the business of the Association.

FUNDS.

Expenses of Management.—In order to defray the expenses of the Central Committee, each Trade in the Association shall contribute one penny per month for each paying member, which sum shall be remitted quarterly to the General Secretary. Should any surplus funds accrue from these sub-scriptions, the Central Committee shall have the option of reducing the subscription, or applying the said surplus in payment of the expenses of the annual Conference, which, unless thus provided for, shall be borne by the trades who return delegates.

Remittances.—The monthly subscriptions and levies shall be collected by the local officers of each Trades' Union in the Association, and forwarded by them to the Central Committee, or to such places as they may direct.

LOCAL AGENTS.

District Committees and Secretaries.—Trades' Unions in the Association may form district committees composed of delegates from their respective bodies, and the committee thus formed shall appoint a Secretary, through whom all communications to the General Secretary shall be made. Such Secretaries shall become honorary members of the Central Committee.

Agents.—The Central Committee may appoint agents, members of any society belonging to the Association, and empower them to visit Trades' Unions, for the purpose of explaining the objects of the Association, and urging its claims on the support of the industrious classes; and also to visit places where disputes exist between masters and men, to collect information for the Central Committee, and, if empowered by them, to mediate between the contending parties.

ACCOUNTS AND STATISTICAL RETURNS.

Quarterly Reports.—Each trade shall quarterly make up reports of the following matters to the Central Committee—namely, a statement of the number of paying members on the books of the society, the average number out of employment during the quarter, the rate of wages, and such other information as the Central Committee may request or need, to enable it to discharge its duties efficiently.

General Reports.—The Central Committee shall make the following reports and statements of accounts for the information of the trades:—

1. A quarterly account of the receipts and disbursements of the Central Committee.
2. Half-yearly statistical tables of the state of the Association, con-formable to the reports received from the trades.
3. An annual cash balance-sheet to be made up to Lady-Day, and laid before the Conference at its annual session.

And such quarterly accounts shall be made up to Lady-Day, Midsummer, Michaelmas, and Christmas, and shall include the accounts of the trades for the preceding quarter.

Authentication.—Every such periodical account shall be attested by two auditors to be appointed by the Conference, and counter-signed by the General Secretary. All drafts on the treasurer shall be signed by the secretary, and countersigned by the president, or, in his absence, by the vice-president.

T. S. DUNCOMBE, President.
T. BARRATT, Secretary,
30, Hyde-street, Bloomsbury.

London, Aug. 2nd, 1845.

The following are the Names, Addresses, and Occupations of the Members of the Central Committee :—

T. S. Duncombe, Esq., M.P., President, 3F Albany, Piccadilly.
Mr. J. Bush, Carpenter, Vice-President, 1, York-street, York Road.
George Bird, Esq., Surgeon, 7, Union Place, New Road, Marylebone, Treasurer.
Mr. Dunning, Bookbinder, Magnet Coffee-house, Drury-lane, London.
Mr. Allen, Tinplate Worker, 88, Cannon-street, City, London.
Mr. James, Boot and Shoe maker, 3, Fleur-de-lis Court, Gray's Inn-lane, London.
Mr. W. J. Young, Carpenter, 33, Park-street, Dorset-square, London.
Mr. F. Green, Morocco Leather Dresser, 37, Theobald-street, New Kent Road, London.
Mr. Robert Mullen, Woolcomber, Syrrel Court, Bradford, Yorkshire.
Mr. John Rogers, Carpenter, 14, Jacob-street, St. Phillips, Bristol.
Mr. William Felkin, Framework Knitter, Wheatsheaf, Stockwell Gate, Mansfield, Nottinghamshire.
Mr. W. Palmer, Plasterer, 84, Devonshire-street, Hulme, Manchester.
Mr. Lynes, Sik Weaver, White Lion Court, Magdalen-street, Norwich.
Mr. Berry, Coal Miner, Scholfield-lane, Wigan, Lancashire.

AUDITORS.

Mr. J. T. Gimblett, 3, Howick Terrace, Vauxhall Bridge Road, London.
Mr. Wm. Robson, 14, Richard's-place, Haggerstone Bridge, London.

List of Trades represented in the July Conference, 1845.

LONDON DELEGATES.

Trades.	Names and Addresses of Delegates.
Bookbinders	Mr. Dunning, Magnet Coffee-house, Drury-lane
Boot and Shoemakers	Mr. W. Clark, 27, Rupert-street, Haymarket
,,	Mr. James, 9, Fleur-de-lis-court, Gray's Inn- lane
,,	Mr. Robson, 14, Richard's-place, Haggerstone
,,	Mr. Storey, 5, John-street, Hanway-street, Oxford-st.
Carpenters	Mr. W. J. Young, Park-street, Dorset-square
,,	Mr. Wade, Lambeth-square, Lambeth
,,	Mr. Bush, 1, York-street, York-road, Lambeth
,,	Mr. Read, ditto
,,	Mr. Seccombe, 96, Great Suffolk-street, Borough
,,	Mr. Gimblett, 3, Howick-terrace, Vauxhall-bridge-road
Carvers and Gilders	Mr. Williams, Green Man, Berwick-street, Oxford-st.
Cigar Makers	Mr. Aarons, 4, Palmer-street, Spitalfields
Goldbeaters	Mr. Hutchins, 105, Shoe-lane, Fleet-street
Morocco Leather Dressers	Mr. F. Green, 37, Theobald-street, New Kent-road
Plasterers	Mr. Firth, Bridge-place, Lower-road, Deptford
Silk Hatters	Mr. L. Jones, 16, Chapel-place, Long-lane, Bermondsey
,,	Mr. Arch, 24, Granby-street, Waterloo-road
,,	Mr. Bond, 8, Riley-park, Abbey-street, Bermondsey
Tinplate Workers	Mr. W. Allen, 88, Cannon-street, City.

PROVINCIAL DELEGATES.

Belper Nailmakers .... Mr. J. Gregory, 4, North Belper, Derbyshire
" Mr. J. Whitehurst, Belper
Bradford Woolcombers ......"Mr. Mullen, Syrrel-court, Bradford, Yorkshire
" Mr. White, 55, Cross-street, Manchester-road, Bradford, Yorkshire
Bury Builders .... Mr. Smith, Bolton-street, Bury, Lancashire
Birkenhead Bricklayers ...... Mr. Wilson, 11, Rose Cottages, Limekiln-lane, Tran-
mere, Cheshire
Ditto Plasterers .... Mr. Cooper, 1, Queen-st., North Birkenhead, Cheshire
Bristol Trades .... Mr. J. Rogers, 14, Jacob-street, St. Phillips, Bristol
Crayford Block Printers ...... Mr. Kenyon, Crayford, Kent
Lancashire ditto .... Mr. Stephenson, Blackburn-st., Accrington, Lancashire
Lancashire Miners .... Mr. Pasquel, Doffcocker, near Bolton
" Mr. Berry, Scholfield-lane, Wigan
Ditto Cotton Spinners .... Mr. Gregory, Dawson-lane, Little Bolton
Liverpool Bricklayers' La-
bourers...................... Mr. Young, "The Cabbage," Scotland-place, Liverpool
" Mr. H. Rooney, ditto
MansfieldFrameworkKnitters Mr. W. Felkin, Wheatsheaf, Stockwell-gate, Mansfield
Manchester Dressers & Dyers Mr. Bradley, at Mr. Seir's, 22, Charlton-st., Manchester
Ditto Associated Trades ...... Mr. Roberts, 3, Salford-street
Ditto Plasterers .... Mr. W. Palmer, 84, Devonshire-street, Hulme
Ditto Bricklayers' Labourers Mr. Grady, Red Bull, Mason-street, Manchester
Ditto Boiler Makers .... Mr. Macnamara, Star and Garter, Arbour-square, Com-
mercial-road
Maidstone Papermakers...... Mr. Baker, Springfield Mills, Maidstone
" Mr. Mason, Maidstone
Norwich Trades .... Mr. Lynes, White-lion-court, Magdalen-street, Norwich
Oxford Boot & Shoemakers. Mr. Pavitt, 46, Friars-street, St. Ebbs, Oxford
Rochdale Trades .... Mr.A.Crabtree,Clock-face Inn,Blackwater-st., Rochdale
Staffordshire Potters.......... Mr. W. Evans, Brunswick-street, Shelton, Staffordshire
Potteries
Surrey Blockprinters .... Mr. John Dale, Block-printer, Victory Inn, Merton
" Mr. Bulger, ditto, ditto
Yarmouth Trades .... Mr. Royall, at Mr. Hoy's, News agent, Charlotte-street,
Yarmouth

IV.

FINANCIAL REPORT OF THE CENTRAL
COMMITTEE OF THE UNITED BUILDINGS' TRADES,

From June 26th, to November 26th, 1845.

INCOME.

			£	s.	d.
June 26th, Cash received from Labourers, for 600 Cards and Rules, at 2d.			5	0	0
— Cash from Chestmakers, 120 ditto			1	0	0
— " Plumbers, 57 ditto			0	9	6
— " Joiners, 400 ditto			3	6	8
— " Bricklayers, 424 ditto			3	10	8
— " Slaters, 67 ditto			0	11	2
— " Central Committee of Stockport, 1000 ditto			3	0	0
28, " Plumbers, 13 ditto			0	2	2
Sep. 10, " Treasurer, ditto			0	12	3
17, " Ditto, ditto			0	6	6
20, Borrowed from Plumbers			2	0	0
Oct. 1, Cash from Treasurer			0	12	0
— " Joiners for 200 Cards and Rules			1	13	4
Carried forward			0	0	0

42

Brought forward .... | £. s. d. | 0 0 0

Levy in aid of Plumbers' Strike.

			£	s.	d.
Oct. 3,	Cash from	Slaters, 67 at 6d...........................	1	13	6
—	,,	Plumbers, 80 ditto........................	2	0	0
—	,,	Labourers, 600 ditto	15	0	0
—	,,	Joiners, 562 ditto	14	1	0
—	,,	Chestmakers, 120 ditto...................	3	0	0
—	,,	Bricklayers, 500 ditto	12	10	0
—	,,	Treasurer, ditto	20	6	0
6	,,	Slaters, for 30 Cards and Rules	0	5	0
—	,,	Plumbers, 30 ditto	0	5	0
8	,,	Treasurer............................	0	5	0

Levy in aid of the Plumbers' Strike.

				£	s.	d.
Oct. 10,	Cash from	Joiners, 562 at 6d. each................		14	1	0
—	,,	Chestmakers, 120 ditto		3	0	0
—	,,	Labourers, 600 ditto		15	0	0
—	,,	Plumbers, 70 ditto		2	5	0
—	,,	Slaters, 87 ditto		2	3	6
15,	,,	Treasurer, ditto		28	0	0
17,	,,	Ditto, ditto..........................		0	14	0
—	,,	Joiners, 562 ditto		14	1	0
—	,,	Slaters, 87 ditto		2	3	6
—	,,	Plumbers, 72 ditto		2	6	0
—	,,	Labourers, 600 ditto		15	0	0
22,	,,	Bricklayers, 500 for two weeks		25	0	0
24,	Received from Treasurer			0	19	0
—	Levy from	Joiners, 562 at 2d......................		4	13	8
—	,,	Plumbers, 75 ditto		0	15	10
—	,,	Slaters, 87 ditto		0	14	6
—	,,	Labourers, 600 ditto		5	0	0
—	,,	Chestmakers, 120 ditto		1	0	0
—	,,	Ditto, due on the 17th September		3	0	0
29,	,,	Treasurer, ditto		0	10	0
—	,,	Ditto ditto		9	8	5½
Nov. 4,	,,	Bricklayers, due on the 24th of Oct. at 2d.		4	3	4
5,	,,	Treasurer		0	12	5
8,	,,	Ditto		6	4	6
—	,,	Labourers, Nag's Head Society, for 250 Cards and Rules, at 2d		2	1	8
11,	,,	Plumbers, 30 ditto		0	5	0
12,	,,	Joiners, 562 at 1d.		2	6	10
—	,,	Labourers, Nag's Head Society, 250 at 1d.		1	0	10
—	,,	Bricklayers, 500 ditto...................		2	1	8
—	,,	Slaters, 87 ditto		0	7	3
—	,,	Chestmakers, 120 ditto		0	10	0
19,	,,	Plumbers, 95 ditto		0	7	11
21,	,,	Treasurer, ditto		2	1	0
25,	,,	Ditto, ditto		0	14	5
26,	,,	Ditto, ditto		4	14	5
	,.	Ditto, ditto		0	5	6½

Carried forward .... | | 0 0 0

	£.	s.	d.
Brought forward	0	0	0

Cash due to Central Committee.

	£	s.	d.
By Sawyers	38	5	2
,, Painters	9	11	3
,, Brickmakers	7	0	0
,, Labourers at the Red Bull	2	10	0
,, Labourers at the Nag's Head	20	16	8
	£178	3	1

Treasurer's Account.

	£	s.	d.
Cash paid to Treasurer	76	5	3
,, Received	76	3	6
Cash in treasurer's hand	0	1	9
	£269	2	0

EXPENDITURE.

			£.	s.	d.
May 29th,	Paid	for Rent of Carpenters' Hall, for Aggregate Meeting in passing laws	1	17	6
July 3rd,	,,	for Printing 4000 Cards and Rules	10	0	0
—	,,	for a Set of Books for Central Committee	0	17	0
17th,	,,	to James Taylor, for revising Rules and numbering Cards, and waiting on Printer	0	6	0
—	,,	to James Maxwell, for ditto	0	3	6
29th,	,,	to one Delegate for attending Committee	0	0	6
Aug. 7th,	,,	to two ditto ditto ditto	0	1	0
14th,	,,	to six ditto ditto ditto	0	3	0
21st,	,,	to five ditto ditto ditto	0	2	6
28th,	,,	to William Hulmes, for pens and ink	0	2	0
Sept. 4th,	,,	to seven Delegates, for attending Committee	0	3	6
—	,,	to Charles Simms, and for Stationery	0	8	1½
10th,	,,	to William Hulme, for Rent of Meeting-room, and acting as Secretary from the 17th of July to the 4th of Sep., 1845	0	7	0
—	,,	to Rent of Meeting-room and Postage.	0	1	3
—	,,	to eight Delegates for attending Committee	0	4	0
—	,,	to Treasurer	2	11	6
17th,	,,	for Rent of Meeting. for two nights at 9d.	0	1	6
—	,,	to Wm. Hulme and Jas. Taylor, for a Deputation	0	2	0
—	,,	to six Delegates for attending Committee	0	3	
18th,	,,	for Paper and Postage	0	0	8
20th,	,,	to John Sharples and Philip Welch, for three days' wages and expenses for waiting on the Master Plumbers respecting the advance of the Plumbers' wages	2	2	0
—	,,	for Inkstands	0	1	4
Oct. 1st,	,,	to Delegates for attending Committee, 3 nights..	0	10	0
—	,,	to Thomas Railton and John Roberts, for a Deputation to Chestmakers' Society, on the 19th September	0	2	0
		Carried forward	0	0	0

			£.	s.	d.
		Brought forward	0	0	0
Oct, 1st,	„	to Treasurer	1	13	4
—	„	Ditto	48	4	6
—	„	to eight Delegates for attending Committee	0	4	0
—	„	to Plumbers, for fifty men on strike three days, one man 1¼ days	19	1	3
—	„	for getting two Tramps out of Town	0	5	6
—	„	to seven of Strike Committee, three days at 6d.	0	10	6
3rd,	„	sending a man to Alderley Edge to stop blacks.	0	5	0
—	„	ten Delegates for attending Committee	0	5	0
6th,	„	nine ditto ditto ditto	0	4	6
10th,	„	to Plumbers, for fifty-three men on strike 6 days.	39	15	0
—	„	to Bricklayers, one man 5⅓ days	0	13	9
—	„	Labourers, two men 6 days, and one man ½ a day	1	11	3
—	„	to Masons, one man 6 days. }			
—	„	ditto one man 1½ days }	0	18	9
—	„	to Joiners, two men 6 days, and one man 3½ days	1	18	9
—	„	to Plasterers, two men 6 days, and one man 2 days	1	15	0
—	„	to seven of Strike Committee men, 6 days at 6d. each	1	1	0
—	„	for 1000 Placards to stop men from coming into the town	3	12	0
—	„	for 3 days' wages, and expenses of Philip Welch for bringing out the men	1	1	0
—	„	Incidental in getting the men out	1	1	9
—	„	for getting Tramps out of town	2	6	6
—	„	for three Delegates to Liverpool and Birkenhead, with placards to stop the fifty men advertised in the *Liverpool Mercury*	6	17	4
—	„	to Treasurer, ditto	1	6	6½
—	„	to Bricklayer and Labourer, due on 2nd Oct	0	6	10½
—	„	to eight Delegates for attending Committee	0	4	0
13th,	„	to twelve ditto ditto ditto	0	6	0
15th,	„	to ten ditto ditto ditto	0	5	0
—	„	for Rent of Room, for four nights at 9d. each night	0	3	0
17th,	„	to eleven Delegates attending Committee	0	5	6
—	„	to Plumbers, for twenty-six men on strike 6 days, and one man 1½ days	19	13	9
—	„	to Bricklayers, one man 4½ days	0	11	3
—	„	to Labourers, one man 4½ days	0	11	3
—	„	to Masons, one man 5 days	0	12	6
—	„	to Joiners, one man 6 days	0	15	0
—	„	for getting eight Men out of Town	3	15	4
—	„	for four Delegates to Leeds, Derby, Birmingham, and Sheffield, &c., with Placards to stop the Men advertised in the *Liverpool Mercury*	12	9	7
—	„	for seven Strike Committee, 6 days at 6d. each	1	1	0
—	„	for Incidentals in getting Men out	1	19	11¼
—	„	to Plumbers' Money borrowed on 20th Sept.	2	2	0
—	„	to Treasurer	14	14	4½
—	„	to Bricklayers' Delegates, due on 8th Sept.	0	1	0
20th,	„	to eight Delegates for attending Committee	0	4	0
22nd,	„	to ten ditto ditto ditto	0	5	0
—	„	to Philip Welch and William Dean, one day's Wages and Expenses, for waiting on Samuel P. M. Slater, respecting the Communionist working in his employment	0	14	0
		Carried forward	0	0	0

			£.	s.	d.
		Brought forward	0	0	0
Oct. 23rd,	,,	for Paper for the Central Committee	0	0	6
24th,	,,	for ten Delegates attending Committee	0	5	0
—	,,	to James Taylor, one day's wages and expenses for getting the men to work at the jobs of Messrs. Howard and Atkinson	0	7	0
—	,,	to Plumbers, for 14 men on strike six days, and one man 4½ days	11	1	3
—	,,	to Strike Committee, for six days at 6d. each	0	16	0
—	,,	to getting men out of town	0	13	0
—	,,	to Incidentals	0	1	0
—	,,	to Philip Welch, four days' wages and expenses to stop any job where blacks are working	1	8	0
—	,,	to one Bricklayer, on strike one day	0	2	6
—	,,	to one labourer, half day	0	1	3
—	,,	to one Joiner, on strike two days	0	5	0
—	,,	Cash to Messrs. Metcalf and Lavender, for a seal for the Central Committee	0	10	0
25th,	,,	for Postage	0	0	1
—	,,	to Treasurer	0	4	0
29th,	,,	to twelve Delegates for attending Committee	0	6	0
—	,,	to John Sellers and James Taylor, for one day's wages and expenses in waiting on Parkinson and Pink, respecting the dispute of the bricklayers	0	14	0
—	,,	to John Sharples and James Taylor, for a deputation to the Nag's Head Society of Labourers, respecting the levy	0	2	0
—	,,	to Thomas Railton, for making a Box for the Central Committee	1	0	0
—	,,	to Treasurer	4	3	4
Nov. 13th,	,,	to Plumbers, for eight men on strike six days, and one man 1½ days	6	3	9
—	,,	to Strike Committee, for six days	0	15	0
—	,,	to Incidentals	0	5	8½
14th,	,,	to twelve Delegates attending Committee	0	6	0
—	,,	for expenses of the Central Committee Meeting at Blackmoor's Head	0	5	11
5th,	,,	to Thomas Railton and Philip Welch, half a day's wages and expenses in waiting on Mr. Beaver, respecting piece-work of the Joiner	0	7	0
—	,,	to thirteen Delegates attending Committee	0	6	6
—	,,	for Postage	0	0	1
8th,	,,	to Plumbers, for five men on strike six days, and one man three days	4	2	6
—	,,	to Strike Committee, for six days each	0	15	0
—	,,	for getting three men out of town	0	11	0
—	,,	Incidental on getting blacks out	0	2	6
11th,	,,	to William Goodwin, half day's wages	0	3	6
—	,,	to Jesse Boyne, one day's wages and expenses, in waiting on Mr. Wilson, respecting the dispute of the Bricklayers about an apprentice	0	7	0
—	,,	to fourteen Delegates for attending Committee	0	7	0
—	,,	to Treasurer	1	2	10
—	,,	for Expenses of Meeting at Blackmoor's Head	0	5	6
—	,,	to Hugh M'Henry, for a Deputation to Plumbers on the 1st November	0	1	0
			—	—	—
		Carried forward	0	0	0

			£.	s.	d.
		Brought forward	0	0	0
12th,	,,	to Thomas Railton and Jesse Bryne, one day's wages and expenses, in waiting on the master Bricklayers, respecting the Labouring	0	14	0
—	,,	to fifteen Delegates attending Committee	0	7	6
—	,,	to Plumbers, for three men on strike 6 days, and one man 5 days	2	17	6
—	,,	Committee Expenses for six days..............	0	3	6
—	,,	for getting two tramps out of Town	0	5	0
—	,,	Incidentals	0	2	0
—	,,	Postage	0	1	2
—	,,	to Treasurer	2	4	10
14th,	,,	for Letter-book and Stamps	0	2	6
15th,	,,	for Postage ....,..............	0	0	7
19th,	,,	for sixteen Delegates attending Committee	0	8	0
—	,,	to Plumbers, two men on strike 6 days, and one man 1 day	1	12	6
—	,,	Expenses ,...................................	0	0	6
21st,	,,	for Expenses of Meeting at the Blackmoor's Head	0	6	11
—	,,	to fifteen Delegates attending Committee	0	7	6
23rd,	,,	Postage ... :.............	0	1	2
24th,	,,	for Expenses of Meeting at the Blackmoor's Head	0	3	8
—	,,	ditto ditto ditto	0	6	9
—	,,	to Thomas Railton and Hugh M'Henry, for ¾ day's Wages and Expenses, in waiting on Messrs. Eastwood and Travo, respecting the dispute of the Chestmakers	0	10	6
—	,,	to Treasurer for his Salary....................	0	15	0
—	,,	to Secretary, ditto	1	7	0
—	,,	to Plumbers, for two men on strike 3 days......	0	15	0
—	,,	to fourteen Delegates attending two nights......	0	14	0
28th,	,,	to one Delegate attending Committee..........	0	0	6
—	,,	to James Taylor and Hugh M'Lenny, for a Deputation to the Labourers, Nag's Head Society, on the 22nd November....................	0	2	0
26th,	,,	to seven Delegates for attending Committee	0	3	6
—	,,	to Paper for Balance Sheet...................	0	0	9
			£269	5	0

Audited and found correct,
JOHN SELLERS,
GEORGE NEWTON.

V.

THE LAWS, INCOME, AND EXPENDITURE OF THE BUILDING TRADES' UNION.

We have before us a copy of the " Rules for the Government of the United Building Trades' Mutual Protection Society of Manchester, Salford, and their vicinities," with an introduction by " The central committee," in which they say, " we have felt it imperative upon us to adopt some measures for our mutual preservation and protection. These, embodied in the following rules, appear to us the best means that can be adopted at present for resisting injustice and oppression, when attempted to be practised upon us by unprincipled employers," &c. The rules are nineteen in number, and too long for publication entire. We give the following abstract of them, distinguishing the passages quoted, by inverted commas:—

1. "That this society shall consist of operatives in union of every branch belonging to the building trades, and be established for the mutual protection and assistance of each other, in every case of strike or turn-out, arising from unjust encroachments by unprincipled employers, and for the *prevention of non-unionists encroaching on our respective employments.*"—2. Vests the government in a committeee formed of one delegate from each trade, serving three months, meeting once a fortnight, "to hear all reports," &c. In case of strike, or other business of importance, two delegates from each trade to form the committee, and meet as often as they find necessary; each delegate getting 6d. for every meeting he attends.—3. A president, chosen from the delegates, is to hear all motions for any new orders or regulations, to sign all minutes of proceedings, and all orders of cash from the treasurer. — 4. A secretary, appointed from the delegates, to continue in office so long as he gives satisfaction; to attend all meetings, record the names of the delegates present, and keep minutes of all proceedings and all accounts, documents, &c., as required by the delegates, and to do all necessary writing; salary, what he and the delegates agree upon; and his trade to send another delegate in his place, the secretary having no vote.—5. The treasurer is to be a fit person to hold any sum that may be placed in his possession, and, when required, to find two bondsmen for its security; to keep an account of all monies received and paid by him; but not to pay any without an order signed by the president and secretary; salary, what he and the delegates agree.—6. Each delegate to enter in a book all necessary proceedings, and report them at every meeting of his respective [trade] society; the book to be transferred to his successor.—7. "That each trade shall keep its own funds for the support of this society, and shall pay the amount of levy that may be laid on by the delegates, every Friday night, to the secretary and treasurer."—8. "That in case of any dispute between any of the trades in connection with this society and their employers, the trade in question shall inform the secretary of the delegates, who shall summon the delegates to attend a meeting, when parties from the complaining trade shall attend and state the nature of their dispute, and if it be to the satisfaction of the delegates, they shall appoint two of the delegates to go with two of the complaining trades to the said employer, to see if they can settle the dispute pending. If not to the satisfaction of the said trade, the delegates shall call a meeting of their respective trades, and lay the nature of dispute before them for their consideration, and must bring the number of their respective members for and against the support of the same. And if the majority of the whole of the trades are not satisfied with the terms offered by the said employer, it shall be left with the delegates to decide what plan to adopt; whether *to call the complaining trade, or any other trade, or the whole of the trades, from the said employer, or his sub-contractors ;* but if the majority of the whole of the trades are satisfied with the terms offered by the said employer, the complaining trade must accept such terms, or they will not be supported by this society. And if at any time during any strike the delegates think it necessary to negotiate with the employers in the strike pending, they must lay the result of the said negotiation before the aggrieved trade, and if it be satisfactory to the said trade, the strike shall terminate on that negotiation; but if the aggrieved trade is not satisfied with the result of the said negotiation, the delegates shall lay it before their separate trades as above stated." 9. Delegates may appoint a committee of two or more members of each trade, to sit daily, and call the names of the men on strike, at 9½ a.m., and 3½ p.m. Any man not answering shall not be paid for the time he neglects. "The committee must send their roll-list, together with the list of incidental expenses they have incurred *in getting tramps out of*

the town, that have come to work in the places of the men on strike, every afternoon, at five o'clock, to the secretary, so that he can give in the exact amount of levy required every Wednesday night to the delegates." Each member of this committee to have 6d. per day over his strike pay —10. Each member of the society to receive 15s. a week when on strike, or 2s. 6d. per day, &c.—11. The delegates of each trade to bring its numbers, so that the levy may be made equally, according to the numbers given ; and any trade sending a false statement to be fined.—12. "That if, at the time of any strike' there should be any non-unionists in the employment where such strike takes place, they shall, providing they strike with the men belonging to this society, receive the same amount of pay, but they *must enter their respective trade society*, or they will not be supported by this society."—13. "That if any men, during any strike in connection with this society, go to work in the employment where such strike is pending, in opposition to the rules of this society, *their names shall be obtained and circulated in the various Building Trades' Societies throughout the kingdom.*"—14. A quarterly report to be published of income and expenditure, and proceedings of the Delegates' Committee ; during a strike, the report to he published monthly, if necessary.—15. " That, in case of emergency, the delegates have *to send parties into the country to stop men on strike*," the parties sent to be men on strike, if qualified ; otherwise to be selected for the purpose.—16. " Each trade shall send a list of the employers for whom non-unionis's are working, and the number of men employed of other trades, belonging to this society, where such non-unionists are working ; and such means will be adopted as the delegates may deem practicable, to *induce them to join their respective trade society*."— 17. " That no act of violence, threat, intimidation, or abusive language, towards any non-unionist, or other person opposed to this society, will be in any way countenanced by this society ; the trade so offending will be subject to a fine ; and this society will not screen any person or persons from the punishment justly due for such offence."—18. Each member of a trade society, in connection with this union, to have a card of membership. 19. In disputes not provided for by the rules, the delegates to legislate ; but not to have power to add to, take from, or alter any rule, without the sanction of a majority of the whole of the trades, after one month's notice. Any trade breaking the rules, to be dealt with according to the decision of a majority of the whole of the trades.

Such is a summary of the rules of a society, the very first of which, in the passage we have marked in *italics*, stamps it an illegal association. According to that rule, it is a society for preventing workmen from obtaining employment, unless they will submit to the rules which it prescribes. It is a convention of delegates from different building trades' unions or societies, for the purpose of making levies, and thus supporting any or all these trades during strikes ; and even to declare when a particular trade shall strike, or, as the 8th rule terms it, " to call the complaining trade or any other trade, or the whole of the trades, from the employer or his sub-contractors." Yet these men deny the charge of dictation to employers. The other duties of the delegates' committee appear to be to get tramps out of town ; to circulate in the various building trades' societies throughout the kingdom as " illegal men," the names of any men who go to work for any employer against whom a strike is pending. Yet they deny using any restrictions on the employer, or over-awing or intimidating the workmen. Picquets are now placed near the premises of various employers ; and yet the men deny all intimidation and over-awing of the workmen who are willing to work, and all interference with, dictation to, or restriction of, the employer, as to the mode in which he shall carry on his business. The 15th rule is not very clear ; but it hints at the practice of sending men into the country to stop men on strike ; and the 16th rule intimates darkly that such means as the delegates may deem " practicable," will be adopted to " induce" non-unionists to join the trade society. After all this, we do not attach any weight to the 17th rule, which may be convenient to cite in a court of justice, to show that the union discountenances all violence and intimidation; but it is clearly contrary both to the spirit of the rules, and to the practice of some, at least, of the turn-outs in building trades.

VI.

I had men working at Messrs. ———'s for many weeks, when about Christmas last I sent two fresh hands to assist in finishing the job, one of them I had taken on as a gas-fitter only; he had been with me about two months, (I knew nothing whatever of his being a plumber). The same day that these two men went to the warehouse, a notice was given to Mr. ———, jun., that if my men continued, they (the joiners and plasterers) must quit the premises. I went up about four o'clock in the afternoon, to enquire what my hands had done amiss, when Mr. ——— called into the counting-house, a joiner of the name of Clarkson, who appeared to be the chief; we had barely just entered the office when a plasterer and his labourer opened the door and walked in, to be witnesses of what was passing. I asked ——— what was wrong, he pulled a paper out of his pocket, and read over the names of five or six of my men who, he said, would not be allowed to work any where unless they entered the club. I then remarked that I had other hands that I would send to finish the job who were not plumbers, and whose names he had not on the proscribed list, he said it was no use, that mine was an illegal shop; I did not give the wages, &c. I replied that I did give the full demand that the men had asked, but that I would use my own discretion as to what men I employed; that it mattered not to me whether the men were in a union or no, so that they did their duty to me, yet that I would not be dictated to by any union or club whatever, in the choice of my hands. At this stage of the business the plasterers' labourer, an Irishman, bawled out that if my men did join the union, I must bring a ticket from their secretary to say that I was a legal man myself. The next morning I sent other hands, when a joiner immediately gave notice that no one from my shop would be allowed to work there, or at least if they did, they (the joiners and plasterers) would all leave the building. Another man told one of my apprentices, who had worked there some time, that he had a good mind to throw a bucket of water (which he then held in his hands) upon him, for bringing any of ———'s men there. In some few days after this, I had an interview with a deputation from the plumbers' society, and again a second interview in about four days afterwards, when the disputed point between me and the union was adjusted, by their allowing me to make choice of my own hands, and it was then understood that if the new hands I had got would join the club, all opposition against my shop would be abandoned. I named the subject to my men, when they agreed, for the sake of peace, to join, although the society condemned them in a fine of £2. each for daring to work without their consent. After I had come to a fair understanding (as I thought) with the deputation, I intended the day but one following, to send my men again to work, but the day after the final interview, Mr. ———. sen., called upon me with the following copy of a resolution of the committee of the union, with their seal or stamp upon it, and which he had obtained from the joiners to whom it was sent:—

VII.

January 8th, 1846.
To the various building Trades working at Mr. ———'s warehouse, Church-street, Manchester.

c

Gentlemen,—This is to certify that the dispute between Mr. ——
is not settled until such time as the men now in his employment joins the
plumbers' society. We have had an interview with Mr. ——, and has
agreed with him that everything will be right if his men will comply with
the rules of our society, and that he has promised to mention it to them,
and as soon as they comply we will inform you, and until such time we hope
you will stick to the original agreement.

Yours,

THE OPERATIVE PLUMBERS AND GLAZIERS OF MANCHESTER.

VIII.

RATES OF WAGES.

The following is a statement of the average wages of good carpenters and
bricklayers in the towns mentioned:

Nottingham	20s. to 22s.	per week.
Derby	21s. to 24s.	,,
Newark	20s.	,,
Birmingham	24s.	,,
Bath	18s. to 20s.	,,
Cheltenham and Leamington	20s.	,,
Gloucester	18s. to 20s.	,,
Worcester	18s. to 20s.	,,
Bolton	24s.	,,
Ashton	24s. to 25s.	,,
Bradford	21s. to 22s.	,,

It will, perhaps, be remembered that the terms offered by the Manchester
Masters for good workmen, and refused by the turn-outs, were as follow:—

Carpenters and Joiners	28s.	per week
Bricklayers	30s.	,,
Plumbers	27s.	,,
Slaters	26s.	,,
Plasterers and Painters	26s.	,,
Labourers	18s.	,,

The wages at Liverpool and Birkenhead have been the same, and were
before the turn-out as below stated:—

Carpenters and Joiners	26s.	per week
Bricklayers	26s.	,,
Labourers	17s.	,,
Masons	26s.	,,
Other trades	26s.	,,

Some of the inferior hands among the joiners have only had 24s., others
27s., and some of the painters and decorators rather more.

IX.

We, the United Building Trades of Manchester and Salford, will not
work at any building or buildings where bricks are larger than the Manchester bricks, as there has been bricks brought from the country that are
larger than the Manchester brickmakers are allowed to make them, to the
injury of the master brickmakers of Manchester and Salford generally.

GENERAL CONCLUDING REMARKS.

I have now laid before the reader, in the statement and appendix which precede, a full and, I believe, an accurate and impartial narrative of the causes and progress of the present turn-out. I sincerely regret that I cannot make it historically complete, by adding the termination to the whole. On reading over the whole case up to this point, I see clearly enough that there are certain passages to which both masters and men will object. The former will accuse me of not speaking in sufficiently strong terms against the injustice, tyranny, and dictatorial interference attempted by the Union. The latter will declare that I have evinced throughout a disposition to look unfavourably upon every measure of the operatives, and to put the best construction upon the conduct of the employers. I can only reply to both parties, that I came to the consideration of the matter in a spirit of impartiality—that have proceeded in the same spirit in which I began, and in which now I form my conclusion. Let me, however, remind all parties, that impartiality does not imply that a man shall have no opinion of his own. It only requires that he should take up a question without bias or prepossession, and treat it with fairness and justice. For myself I confess that the more I have studied this question in all its bearings, the more have I come to a very clear and a very strong opinion. That opinion is decidedly this—that the men turned out unadvisedly and unwisely, and that they have persisted in this false step with an equal disregard of kindliness and gratitude to their employers, and prudence and foresight as regards themselves, their wives, and families. To this false step have they been urged by the suggestions and directions of what I cannot but regard as a most mischievous and detrimental influence—I mean the system of Trades' Unions. I have spoken at length upon this point at the commencement of this pamphlet, and now that I have reached the conclusion of my labours, I would again desire to impress upon the minds of the reader my strong sense of their impolicy, their injustice, and their unconstitutional character. These charges are no coinage of my brain, but are fully established by the contents of these pages. In confirmation of this, I will briefly allude to the documents inserted in the Appendix.

No. 1 is a placard largely distributed in the towns round about Manchester, on the occasion of a recent strike of plumbers in this town.— No. 2 is the notice posted up in the joiners' shops in Manchester, containing the new rules proposed by the Union and acceded to by the masters.—No. 3 is a document of great importance, as proving the revival of a General Trades' Union, upon the extensive basis and organization of that of 1833; having ramifications in every part of the kingdom, and whose powers and duties, as expressed in the rules herein inserted at length, are of the most unguarded character, and open to the most glaring abuse. By one rule, to which I would especially draw attention, any party or political purpose whatever might be forwarded by an appropriation of funds subscribed by the confiding journeymen, through a specious interpretation of the terms in which it is couched. By it the Central Committee are empowered " to promote *all* measures, *political*, social, or educational, which are intended to improve the condition of the working classes." The president of this association is a member of parliament, Mr. T. S. Duncombe, and it is to be hoped that his name has only been appended as a matter of form, and is not to be understood as that of one who is responsible for the principles which are contained in the rules in question.

In the preceding Appendix, No. 4, is an exact copy, errors included, of the " Financial Report of the Central Committee of the United Building Trades, from June 26 to Nov. 26, 1845," and I beg to call particular attention to such items as the following:—

" Oct. 1. For getting two tramps out of town, 5s. 6d. Oct. 3. For sending a man to Alderley Edge, *to stop blacks*, 5s. For 1,000 placards to stop men from coming into the town, £3. 12s.; for three days' wages and expenses of Philip Welch, for bringing out the men, £1. 1s.; incidental in getting the men out, £1. 1s. 9d.; for getting tramps out of town, £2. 6s. 6d.; for three delegates to Liverpool and Birkenhead, with placards to stop the fifty men advertised in the *Liverpool Mercury*, £6. 17s. 4d. Oct. 17. For getting eight men out of town, £3. 15s. 4d.; for four delegates to Leeds, Derby, Birmingham, and Sheffield, &c., with placards to stop the men advertised in the *Liverpool Mercury*, £12. 9s. 7d.; for incidentals in getting men out, £1. 19s. 11½d. Oct. 24. To getting men out of town, 13s.; to Philip Welch four days' wages and expenses *to stop any jobs where blacks were working*, £1. 8s. Nov. 4. For getting three men out of town, 11s.; incidental on getting *blacks* out, 2s. 6d.; for getting two tramps out of town, 5s."

These items alone would be sufficient evidence of the fact that no expense is spared by the union for the carrying out of their designs, and that they do interfere between employers and workmen in a manner which is quite inconsistent with that liberty of the subject so dear to Englishmen.

In the Appendix, No. 5, is an abstract of the " Rules of the United Building Trades Society of Manchester, Salford, and their Vicinity," taken from the *Manchester Guardian* of 21st March, with some remarks by the editor of that journal. The article fully proves that many of the proposed objects of the Trades' Unions are *absolutely illegal*. It will be seen that these are the rules applied to this locality. Those numbered No. 3 in the Appendix are of a General Union extending over the kingdom.

A case of unjust interference of the Union will be found in the Appendix, No. 6, which is the statement of one of the most respectable master plumbers in Manchester, upon whose veracity I can rely. The original letter, a copy of which, marked No. 7, follows his statement, I have in my possession, and it bears the official stamp of the club.

The following instances also illustrate the animus of the proceedings of the turn-outs, and I have taken pains to ascertain that they are correctly stated : Mr. D. Bellhouse had a contract to build a station-house at Ashton-under-Lyne, for the Manchester and Leeds Railway Company, which it was requisite should be completed without delay, on account of the day being fixed for opening the line. It was arranged between the company's manager and Mr. Bellhouse's foreman that some carpenters, in the employ of the company, should be set to finish the work, with the aid of three of Mr. Bellhouse's apprentices. These apprentices were the first to commence annoying the company's workmen, by calling them " knobsticks," &c., and were therefore removed from the job. A number of the turn-outs then went to the place for the express purpose of preventing the carpenters from proceeding with the work; and these men, with the assistance of the masons who were working at the same job, (and who profess to have no connection with the strike,) succeeded in intimidating the workmen, so that on Friday last they came home, and informed the railway company's manager that they *durst* not continue at work. On Saturday, two delegates from the turn-outs waited on the manager, and told him, that if he would employ such men as they would send him, the job might be proceeded with. This the manager would not consent to, and told the delegates that he was sure the company would not countenance such a proceeding. The delegates then said, that if he would get a note from Mr. Bellhouse, stating that *he had given up the job*, the company would be allowed to finish it with their own men. This was acceded to, and the job is now being carried on. On Saturday last, a slater was sent out to the job, but he having come to the town from a distance, and not being connected with the union, was insulted and personally ill-treated, by the masons and two plasterers' apprentices, so that he left the town on Saturday evening. Mr. Bellhouse would have taken proceedings against the men who had ill-used the slater, but the man was so frightened that he would not stay to identify the men. A similar course of proceeding has been resorted to by the turn-outs with respect to another job of Mr. Bellhouse's.

Again, a short time ago, some operative slaters, non-unionists, were employed to slate the new machine-shop belonging to Messrs. Hill and Holmes, in Dawson's-croft, Salford; they were assailed by the turn-outs, who pulled down the ladders by which the building was to be ascended, and would not allow the men to proceed. Some of the master slaters have themselves, with great spirit, finished the work which the operatives were intimidated from doing.

A few days ago, a large mill, now building, in Salford, being stopped, in consequence of the turn-out, the proprietor was applied to by one of the men, who had previously worked on the premises under the contractor, and an agreement was entered into that he should finish the flooring. At the time of making the agreement, he was accompanied by another club man, who required the gentleman to give them a written statement that he had taken the job entirely out of the hands of the former contractor, and that no part of the materials to be used should be procured from him.

No. 8 in the appendix is a statement of wages paid in different parts of the country, from which it will be seen that the wages in Manchester greatly exceed the amounts paid elsewhere.—No. 9 is a specimen of the dictation of the bricklayer's society.

There are several points which I venture to mention here as worthy of consideration, more especially as they immediately affect the public welfare.

One of these points is the pernicious effect which would be exercised upon the general finances of the country, if the ascendancy of the Trades' Unions was to be established, as there could be no security or inducement for a person to lay out his capital in building speculation, on account of the likelihood that an unexpected strike, at the dictation of the Union, might frustrate any plans he had previously laid down.

Another point of importance, in these days of railways, when so many new railroads are in course of completion and projected, consists in the serious effect of a general unexpected rise in the wages for labour, whenever the Union chooses to say the word. The estimates which have been made of the railways now in Parliament, (and upon which estimates the bills will in many cases be obtained,) will prove to be considerably less than the work can be executed for,—and all the calculations which are derived respecting profits upon certain data of expenditure will be fallacious.

Again, it has been seen that, in the strike in 1833, a principal object of the Union was to do away with all contract work whatever; and there is no doubt but that the same unreasonable demand would be made now-a-days, did concessions from the masters lead the men to believe they had power to enforce it. Gentlemen would then be deprived of the advantage of knowing exactly the cost they are likely to go to, at the commencement of any work. I know for a fact, that many persons who contemplated erecting new buildings, or enlarging their present premises, have been deterred from so doing by the strike, and otherwise invested their capital. I believe that much loss is being suffered by those who have buildings in an unfinished state, the use of which they greatly require. The profits of the shopkeepers who supply the workpeople with the necessaries of life are always materially diminished by a lengthened strike; and as the wages of the building operatives, when employed, are sufficiently high to enable them to lay out a tolerable amount weekly upon the comforts as well as the necessaries of life, their cessation from labour, and consequent want of funds will be severely felt.

The Trades' Union can have no influence in raising wages for a permanency to a higher rate than that warranted by the proportion of the number of the operatives to the amount of work required to be done, and if left to be arranged between master and man, the remuneration will always adapt itself to the circumstances of the time,— without the need of the interference of the Union at all in the matter. It is hard to determine whether the proceedings of the Unions are, when acknowledged, a greater tyranny to the masters or to the men; after the fullest consideration of the whole subject, I, however, feel convinced that it is, in reality, the men themselves who most suffer from the galling yoke to which they have submitted themselves. What would be our indignation against that ruler, who should issue his mandate to the effect, that all his subjects were debarred from the privilege of making their own bargains in regard to remunerative employment, and dictate to them that they should not be at all employed, save at a rate which the majority had not the power to deserve? Yet such is the case with the Union;—it passes a resolution that no one shall work, save at a remuneration which only the very best of men can really merit, and tells the man who knows that he is not worthy of the terms, and would willingly accept lower, that he must not work at all unless at the fixed rate. The consequence generally is, that the first-class workmen only get employment, except in very busy times,—the lowest class men being set aside by the masters, on the plea that the same wages must be paid to good and bad workmen. What does all this amount to but a fearful tyranny of numbers over helpless industry? The committee-men, secretaries, and other office-bearers of the clubs, are usually the only parties who derive benefit from the continuance of a strike.

A feature which almost invariably accompanies these strikes is the intimidation which is exercised, with more or less degrees of violence, towards non-unionists and employers. The present strike is not entirely free from these concomitants;* whilst others that preceded it have been marked by incidents which it would be a painful task to recapitulate. I need not do more than just name the events which characterised the sawyers' turn-out, some few years since, at Ashton and the neighbourhood. The records of the criminal courts bear too melancholy an evidence for contradiction. The system of picquets being placed to watch over the workshops of the employers, to report every proceeding to the club, and also at the entrances into the town, to prevent non-unionists from going to work, which is in full operation during strikes, is calculated to do much harm, by destroying mutual good feeling, and engendering suspicion.

Let me recapitulate some of the evils which have been, and still are, the results of a system of combinations among workpeople. It has, then, been proved in this pamphlet, that the dangerous sys-

---

* I have had ocular proofs of this within the last few days.

tem of Trades' Unions is very widely spread. Here we have first a General Association, with head-quarters in London, and a member of parliament as President; which may (as proved by its rules, dated August, 1845,) devote its funds to political, and indeed any other objects. Under the sway of this association, and contributing to its support, are Local Trades' Unions, of every branch, which can, at any moment, with the sanction of the General Association, cause the whole of the operatives in any trade to strike for any object they shall judge expedient, and, if their terms are not acceded to, stop all business in the locality. The existence of such a powerful and irresistible body, and its tyrannical and dictatorial mode of proceeding, is perfectly incompatible with the true interests of both masters and men. If any master engage a workman who refuses to join and subscribe to the Union, the Unionists withdraw from the employ, and persecute the man, until he either joins the club or leaves the town.

The Union dictates how many apprentices shall be taken, how many labourers employed, what hours shall be worked, what wages shall be given, whether piecework shall or shall not be taken, whether contracting shall or shall not be allowed, and, in short, takes upon itself the settlement of matters which it was always considered would be best managed between the employer and the individual employed. Can it then be a matter of wonder, that employers should, at this late hour, resolve to make a determined stand against a combination which arrogates to itself such extraordinary powers? And is it an unreasonable thing, that they ask, in the documents they have issued, the sympathy and co-operation of those who are equally interested with themselves in a fair settlement of the question—the public?

An admirable article appeared, twelve years ago, in one of the leading magazines of the day, in which the writer stigmatizes Trades' Unions in the following strong terms, which past experience has only proved to have been well founded:—" The Trades' Unions have arrayed millions of Englishmen in combination against the authority of the law and the order of society; they threaten to overwhelm industry by the accumulation of numbers, and extinguish opposition by the terrors of self-authorised punishment; laying the axe to the root of the national resources by suspending the labour by which it is created, and locking up the fountains of prosperity by paralysing the capital which must maintain its producers."

Let me earnestly entreat all parties to consider this important subject with impartiality, and with a regard to the best interests of the country, and we feel certain that, having done so, they will come to the conclusion at which I have been forced to arrive, that there are involved in the system and operations of Trades' Unions principles and elements which are incompatible, either with constitutional freedom or national prosperity. In the treatment of this question I have borne in mind that " The courts of reason recognise no difference of persons," and that when we wish to disabuse the minds of men of any thing which we are convinced is erroneous, we must not attempt to do so by careless conclusions or unmeasured condemnation.

CONTENTS.

NOTICE

As circumstances may possibly arise, which will involve the necessity of making a future addendum to this " Statement," any party, possessing documents, the publication of which might be beneficial, would confer a particular obligation by forwarding them, under cover, to " THE COMPILER, &c.," at the Printer's, 50, Market-street, Manchester. Any documents thus received shall be carefully kept, and speedily restored ; they must, however, in all cases, be authenticated by the name and address of the sender, which shall, when required, be considered strictly confidential.

MANCHESTER :

PRINTED AT THE ADVERTISER AND CHRONICLE OFFICE, MARKET-STREET.

REPORT

OF THE

JOURNEYMEN MEMBERS

OF THE

ARBITRATION COMMITTEE,

OR

Conference of Employers and Employed.

TO WHICH IS ADDED,

AN APPENDIX,

CONTAINING THE

SCALES OF PRICES REGULATING NEWS AND PARLIAMENTARY WORK.

LONDON:

PRINTED FOR THE LONDON SOCIETY OF COMPOSITORS.

1847.

—

PRICE THREEPENCE.

THE following Report was read at a Special General Meeting of the Compositors of London, held at the Mechanics' Institution, Tuesday, November 16, 1847, and was received with much approbation by the persons present, at whose particular request it has been printed. After reading the Report, the annexed resolutions of the Employers in respect to the formation of a future Board of Reference (agreed to by them on the same day as the said meeting was held) were read, and directed to be brought before the trade, for consideration and decision upon another occasion:

"That with a view to the settlement of all disputes that may arise between Masters and Journeymen regarding the application of any article of the Scale as amended, a Committee of Reference be appointed, consisting of Twelve Master Printers, of not less than five years' standing in the business, Six to be chosen by the Masters, and Six by the Compositors.

"That if any member of the Committee of Reference shall be a party in any dispute that may be brought before it for adjudication, such member shall withdraw, and not be permitted to deliberate or vote upon that particular case."

The following resolution was afterwards passed by acclamation:

"That the cordial thanks of this meeting be given to the persons forming the journeymen portion of the Arbitration Committee, for their advocacy of the interests of the trade, as also for the satisfactory and highly gratifying report which they have submitted in explanation of their meetings with the employers, and final settlement with them of a mutually-recognised London Scale of Prices."

The undermentioned resolution was also read to the meeting by a member of the Arbitration Committee, and printed at the desire of its framers:

"We (the journeymen on the Arbitration or Conference Committee) take this opportunity of publicly recognising the invaluable labours of your Secretary, Mr. Edwards, and to testify our ample acknowledgment of the services he has rendered to the Trade and his Colleagues during the many sittings of the Conference, throughout which he has not only taken the most prominent part, but invariably displayed the utmost zeal, perseverance, ability, and judgment; and considering it to be but an act of justice to testify to his merits, we feel bound thus publicly to acknowledge them."

REPORT,

&c.

~~~~~~~~~~~~~~~~~

A BRIEF history of the London Compositors' Scale of Prices may not be out of place in introducing to the trade an enlarged edition; as, if given, the past and present will be linked together, and the reader understand what has been accomplished during a period ranging over sixty-two years. From the year 1456, when the art of printing from fusible type was first employed, to 1785, or 329 years, no definite mode of payment to the compositor was practised. That many of them received a fixed price per week, viz. twenty shillings, is pretty certain; and it is equally clear that some were also paid upon the piece, as it is well known that previous to 1785 the price paid for composition of English was 4d. per 1000, long primer 3½d., and brevier 3¼d. In 1785, however, this practice of paying an increased price for the composition of the larger-sized types ceased; for in this year "all founts from English to Brevier inclusive were agreed by the masters to be paid the same price per 1000." It is in 1785 that we first read of anything like a Scale of Prices, and this was originated by the journeymen, who submitted eight propositions to the masters, as the basis of subsequent regulations. Five only out of the eight submitted were agreed to by the employers; and these formed the first Scale of Prices made. Eight years after, viz. in 1793, a conference of masters and men took place, which ended in the ultimate adoption of one out of two propositions submitted by the latter, the second being rejected. In 1800, an advance of one-sixth upon the price per 1000 of the 1785 scale was granted by the masters, who also introduced a second Scale, called the Job Masters' Scale. The following year, 1801, the journeymen resolved upon establishing what

A 2

may be denominated the first trade society; their object being, as they themselves stated, " to correct irregularities, and to bring the modes of charge from custom and precedent into one point of view, in order to their being better understood by all concerned." The custom prior to 1801 for compositors to make known their grievances and wants to the masters, was by signing documents; but now they resolved to establish a different system, for they no doubt saw that going about from house to house to ascertain particular ways of charging was very prejudicial to the interests of all, as each office had its own mode, and consequently it was wholly impossible to determine which of the many practices in being was right. Now in society, compositors acted together, and in less than four years, viz. in 1805, were successful in obtaining an Arbitration Committee, composed of eight masters and eight men, duly authorised by their respective bodies, formed to frame regulations for the future payment of the compositor's work. The result of the labours of this committee has been the basis of charges even up to the present time, now forty-two years. A scale was made, consisting of twenty-seven articles, which in 1810 was slightly altered, and a distinction made, for the first time, between leaded and solid matter. The society of journeymen, it would appear, after having been mainly instrumental in producing so valuable and comprehensive a scale, was allowed to be broken up. Six years after the advance granted in 1810, a reduction of $\frac{3}{4}d$. per 1000 upon reprints was successfully made by the masters. This reduction is remarkable for two things : 1. That sixteen years prior, employers absolutely refused to accede to a proposition put before them by the men, asking for an increase upon manuscript, and at the same time a distinction to be made between manuscript and reprint in the price per 1000. 2. That the document which enforced this alteration of what was called in 1800 " an unjustifiable departure from the established and long-approved principles by which works have been appreciated," was signed by twenty masters only, the men not being consulted, nor their remonstrances heeded when they sought for a definition of the ambiguous term reprint. A strike followed this reduction; but, for want of unanimity, a society or leading power, and the sinews of war—funds, the trade was signally and completely vanquished. From this period, viz. 1816, to the present time, the major part of the profession has been in union, and the scale has not undergone the slightest modification, nor has an attempt been made to violate any one of its twenty-five provisions. But the Scale of 1805-10, with the alteration of 1816, besides admitting of various interpretations as to the real intention of its framers, made no mention of many important matters of daily occurrence to the compositor. In this respect, therefore, it has been often pronounced inadequate to the present wants of the business. In 1834, under the auspices of the late London Union, a commentary was appended to the Scale, which for information and clear reading could not be too highly prized. Subsequently an Appendix was added, exceedingly useful to the compositor. But the Green Book, as this Scale is commonly termed, had one defect; it was the compositors', not the masters' and compositors' book. Master printers would not acknowledge it because journeymen made it ; and thus while it has been a valuable guide to the compositor, it has been of no service to him as an accepted authority by his employer. Numberless disputes have originated upon the wording of the Scale itself ; but those which have produced the most serious consequences, concerned not so much charges that were in the Scale as those which were left out of it. Column-work, table and tabular matter, wrappers, appeal cases, algebra, mathematical works, weekly publications, &c., &c., are not defined in any one of the twenty-five articles ; while their frequent occurrence now-a-days establishes the necessity of simple rules being laid down as a basis for the guidance of both masters and men. The thought seems to suggest itself, that as these kinds of work were unsettled, and dispute upon dispute produced thereby, why was it that another 1805 conference was not called into power ? The answer is, that employers have hitherto declined to take part in such a meeting. Excess of competition, want of fixed rules to frame estimates by, have, fortunately, originated what we cannot but regard as a better feeling : for the proposal to form a joint committee in 1847 did not directly emanate from the journeymen, although heartily supported by them. These few leading particulars, relating to the Scale from its first formation, must suffice, space not permitting further observations to be made upon its history in this report.

We are now brought to that code of laws which will in future regulate the compositors' charges, and be to masters, as well as men, an authority always to be appealed to and mutually recognised. If by any person it is thought that the Scale, as now interpreted, with the matter appended to it, will give a definite price for every description of composition known, such person will be greatly disappointed. The practical compositor knows this is next to impossible ; rules can only be made to govern general principles. This is all the amended Scale will be found to do.

In the month of February last, a deputation from one of the largest offices in the trade waited upon the Committee of the Society, and reported a conversation which they had had with the overseer and their employer, relative to forming an Arbitration Committee, the deputation observing, that if a letter were sent by the trade secretary to the masters' secretary, such letter would be answered, and the Committee, no doubt, afterwards formed. The propriety of sending a letter, expressing the wishes of the trade, to the Masters' Committee, was canvassed at a delegate meeting, the circular, convening the same, calling the attention of the trade to the following proposition, printed in order that chapels and members might consider it previous to the meeting being held: " To consider the propriety of requesting the Master Printers' Association to agree to the formation of an Arbitration Committee, composed of masters and men, to whom every charge *not* decided in the Scale of 1810 shall be submitted for final settlement." This proposition was carried with but two dissentients, and the following letter was sent to J. A. D. Cox, Esq., by the secretary :

Falcon Tavern, Gough Square;
April 22, 1847.

SIR,—I am instructed by the voice of a Delegate Meeting of the London Society of Compositors, respectfully to request you to convene a meeting of the Committee of the Masters' Association, to consider the propriety of forming an Arbitration Committee, consisting of employers and employed, equal numbers, to finally determine all charges not touched upon or clearly defined in the original Scale of 1810, it being the opinion of the said meeting, that it is desirable such a Committee should be formed in the way and for the purpose stated.

I have the honour to be, your most obedient servant,

E. EDWARDS, *Secretary.*

J. A. D. Cox, Esq.

The answer received was in these words :

Great Queen Street; May 24, 1847.

SIR,—I beg to inform you that a Special Meeting of the Committee of the Masters' Association was held yesterday, and your letter of the 22d ultimo laid before them ; whereupon it was resolved, that this Committee, having taken into consideration a communication from Mr. Edwards, as Secretary of the London Society of Compositors, think it desirable, as requested in that letter, that a Committee, consisting of an equal number of masters and compositors should be formed, for the purpose of finally determining all points in dispute, or not touched upon, or clearly defined in the Scale of 1810.

Resolved, That a Committee of eight Masters be appointed to meet an equal number of Compositors for this purpose.

Your obedient servant,

J. A. D. COX.

Mr. E. EDWARDS.

As this letter approved of the formation of the Committee, on June 2, at a Delegate Meeting, the following eight persons were appointed on the part of the trade to serve on the said Committee:— Mr. Adcock, of Clay's; Mr. Craig, of Clowes's; Mr. Feltoe, of Woodfall's; Mr. Ferguson, of Clowes's; Mr. Moses, of Tyler's; Mr. Miller, of Hansard's Old House; Mr. Chapman, of Cox's; and Mr. Edwards, the Secretary. On account of ill-health, Mr. Moses, of Tyler's, was obliged to decline serving; and his place was supplied by Mr. Drew, of Gilbert's. The arrangements for the meeting of the Conference having been determined on by Mr. Cox and Mr. Edwards, the first meeting was held at the Freemasons' Tavern, Great Queen Street, on Friday, July 9; the sittings being continued until November 4. Seventeen meetings with the employers took place, besides many bi-meetings held by the journeymen, discussing the different practices of the trade, and how each alteration proposed would affect the general body. W. Rivington, Esq., occupied the chair; right and left sat R. Clay, Esq.; G. Clowes, Esq.; J. A. D. Cox, Esq.; T. R. Harrison, Esq.; A. Macintosh, Esq.; J. I. Wilson, Esq.; and C. Whittingham, Esq.—the employers. Mr. Drew, of Messrs. Gilbert and Rivington's, occupied the vice-chair, supported by the compositors previously named. Before the business commenced, it was stated that no votes upon any question would be taken, the plan to be adopted was by the employers considering the questions introduced by the journeymen, and *vice versa*, the journeymen the employers. For instance, say a proposition respecting column-work was put forward by the journeymen, accompanied by the reasons calling for its adoption. If the employers approved of it, it was passed; if otherwise, they amended it according to their views, the journeymen either acceding to the alterations proposed, or withdrawing the proposition itself. When any difference of opinion arose, the journeymen had a private retiring-room, where the difference was considered amongst themselves; the employers resorting to the same means when they wished to confer privately with each other. In this way, voting was rendered unnecessary; and a decision arrived at, meeting with the approval of both parties.

In noticing the matter appended to each Article as it will appear in print, concise reasons will be given, in certain cases, why the alterations, &c., have been agreed to. In doing so, we trust every individual present is prepared to hear of concessions made by us, which for years have only been upheld by the simple but important fact, that masters did not wish to put their offices in disorder, consequent upon not agreeing with decisions given by the journeymen's Society. Although many extras have been paid by them during the last thirteen years, in no one instance would these gentlemen permit us to call up the custom of the trade. What had been done, in many respects, they were opposed to ; but acceded to the demands made upon them, because they desired not to run counter with the combination of the men. This is the substance of the invariable remarks of the employers; and not to notice them here would be wrong, since the meetings of this Conference have so practically convinced us of the inestimable value of union, that we unhesitatingly declare our unanimous and sincere conviction, that but for the Society, very many extras which are now secured would not have been countenanced, widely different practices be found existing, and the trade cut short of those privileges which a diligent search clearly proves it has enjoyed for upwards of half a century.

(Each Article, as printed in large type, and forming the 1805-10 Scale, was here read at full length. It cannot be too well understood, that this Scale formed the foundation of the deliberations of the Conference.)

Art. I.—*Vide* Amended Scale, pp. 3-4.

This Art. does not determine the price per 1000 of founts smaller than nonpareil. In future, ruby will be $7\frac{1}{2}d$. solid ; $7\frac{1}{4}d$. leaded ; being one halfpenny increase upon price of nonpareil. Diamond will be 10d. solid, $9\frac{3}{4}d$. leaded, which is a rise of 3d. per 1000 upon nonpareil. Upon all descriptions of work the extra price per 1000 for founts below brevier will be paid. The Article speaks of space lines or leads, and fixes no limit as to their thinness. In most offices 8 to pica leads are deducted for ; and, in some, even 10 to pica, no matter the type they are used in. For years this has been a subject of considerable uneasiness, since injustice was upon the face of it ; for a compositor had to deduct on a pica work just as much as he would if setting nonpareil, 8 to pica leads being used in both. This grievance is remedied, and the sizes of the type will now regulate the reduction for leads 8 and above to the pica, the basis being generally that of one-sixth of the body. Thus, no deduction will be made for leads thinner than 6 to pica on founts larger than long primer, nor for leads thinner than 8 to pica on founts larger than brevier, nor for leads thinner than 10 to pica on founts larger than nonpareil, nor for leads thinner than 12 to pica when used with nonpareil, or smaller type.

Stereotyped matter, when plaster of Paris is used, will be paid, with high spaces, $\frac{1}{4}d$. per 1000 extra ; if with low spaces, $\frac{1}{2}d$. per 1000, as usual ; but where the compositor has not the inconvenience of plaster of

Paris, the extra will not be charged.   This latter remark, however, supposes the compositor to impose his matter in the ordinary way ; but if he have to impose it in small chases, he will then charge 1*s*. per sheet extra for the trouble occasioned by such imposition.

Bastard founts of one remove will be cast up to the depth and width of the two founts to which they belong, as is the custom at present ; and works printed in half-sheets will be cast up in sheets, with their proper extras.

The foregoing has been added to Article I., which now declares the price per 1000 for founts down to diamond, decides what leads shall and shall not be deducted for, and settles the extra for stereotype matter, with the latest improvements therein.   The granting by the masters so clear a definition in respect to leads, of which the Scale is silent, and compositors held liable to deduct for every kind of lead used, induced us to admit that pearl should not be excepted from the rule.

Art. III.—*Vide* Scale, p 5.

This Art. means, that " All works in foreign languages" shall be paid $\frac{1}{2}d$. per 1000 extra down to brevier, and $\frac{3}{4}d$. per 1000 extra for founts smaller than brevier ; but an objection was raised to include, in this word " all," works in the Saxon language set up in ordinary roman type, its peculiarity warranting a higher charge.   The extra labour caused was admitted, and Saxon works, with plain roman type, will be paid $\frac{1}{2}d$. per 1000 extra beyond the price of foreign.   When Saxon or German works are set up in the Saxon or German characters, then one penny extra per 1000 will be charged.   So that a Saxon or German work, in its own character, will be cast up, if in English or brevier, solid, $7\frac{1}{2}d$. per 1000, in minion 8*d*., in nonpareil $8\frac{3}{4}d$.

Art. IV.—*Vide* Scale, p. 5.

Although this Article says " Dictionaries of two or more languages" shall be paid $\frac{1}{4}d$. per 1000 extra, we were successful in getting a just interpretation of these words, rendering Arts. III. & IV. consistent with each other.   Thus, say a German-French dictionary.   This dictionary is in foreign languages, and therefore entitled to be cast up according to Art. III. which says, "all works in foreign languages;" and Art. IV. gives us the right to add to such cast up $\frac{1}{2}d$. per 1000 for dictionary matter. The employers assented to the reasoning mentioned, so that dictionaries wholly in foreign languages will now be paid $\frac{1}{4}d$. per 1000 more than the latter part of the Article, at first sight, seems to allow.

Art. V.—*Vide* Scale, p. 5.

A like anomaly to that just mentioned has also been removed in this Article. The Scale gives no more for a French-German grammar than for an English-French or English-German grammar. The employers at once assented to the alteration proposed, and foreign grammars will now be paid $\frac{1}{4}d$. per 1000 extra beyond the price of foreign works, as settled by Article III.

Art. VI.—*Vide* Scale, p. 6.

Much unpleasantness has been occasioned in consequence of the different meanings given to the words "when cast up at the usual rate," as to whether the extras of the work were to be included, or otherwise. We did not deem it advisable to offer much opposition to the opinion expressed by the employers, as the price stated for Bills in Parliament corroborates their reading; and it was agreed that the words "when cast up at the usual rate" should be interpreted as "including every item of charge."

Art. VII.—*Vide* Scale, p. 6.

Where printed copy is partially introduced, or leads are occasionally used in reviews, magazines, publications, &c., no deduction will have to be made for such print copy or leads, unless with sizes of type leaded throughout according to the plan of the work. Under this Article, publications having two bodies of type in them are to be reckoned. The words "works of a similar description" determine this to be the meaning; so much so, that it was not considered necessary to define what constituted a publication.

Art. VIII.—*Vide* Scale, p. 6.

The words "nearly made up" will be considered to mean two-thirds. Consequently for works for which two-thirds of the letter have been made up without a return, either of its own or a similar work, 1*s*. extra per sheet throughout will be charged. But supposing the work be published in separate volumes, and the letter of the first volume be used for the second, or the second for the third, in such cases the charge for making up letter will not be made beyond the first volume. In all instances, however, it must be distinctly understood, that the letter and leads must be the same kind of letter, the same sized leads; if not, the charge for making up letter will still stand good. Parts of works done at different houses will now be cast up according to their respective merits.

If they consist of a sheet, or less, they will be cast up as jobs ; if over a sheet, and not more than five sheets, as pamphlets.

Art. IX.—*Vide* Scale, p. 6.

The oft-repeated question, " What constitutes the boundary of a sheet of paper ? " has at length been answered. During the last few years, pages which were wont to be called folio have been designated 4to, and quarto 8vo, &c., which is no other than increasing the size and number of the pages in the sheet at the expense of the compositor's extras. A limit is now made as to the size of what shall be termed a sheet. This will be arrived at by ascertaining the number of inches width and breadth the forme when in chase measures, including borders, rules, and inner margins. Thus, take an 8vo outer forme. Measure from the left corner of the first page to the right corner of the fourth page just as imposed, and then measure from the foot of the first page to the foot of the eighth page, inclusive of the white lines, multiplying the dimensions by each other, and should the product be 520, or less, then the sheet shall be considered single ; if exceeding 520, as two single sheets of half the number of pages of which the whole sheet consists, charging a quarto as two sheets of folio, 8vo as two sheets of 4to, &c., as the case may be, the standard being taken from a sheet charged as such during the last twenty years. By this simple method the trade will be protected against the ill-effects of large formes, and also readily ascertain whether the work being performed is imposed in single or double sheets.

Art. X.—*Vide* Scale, p. 7.

No explanation respecting this Article was thought to be necessary.

Art. XI.—*Vide* Scale, pp. 7-8.

We now come to one of the most important alterations made in the newly-arranged Scale, affecting, more or less, every office in the trade, newspapers excepted. It concerns bottom-notes—charging one shilling per sheet throughout a work if two notes occur therein. This and all the other Articles formed the basis of our arguments ; the practice of the trade being valueless to us if opposed to the wording of the Article itself. In March 1840, the Masters' Association issued a circular interpreting the Article to mean two notes for every ten sheets. This led to a Special Delegate Meeting of the trade in the same month, when the trade council caused to be read a report explanatory of the journeymen's reading. This report says:—" The first point to be considered is, whether the right claimed by the trade is authorised by the Scale? Or, in other words, Does the Scale sanction the present custom of the trade in the charge for bottom-notes ?" (p. 2.) This is answered by the trade being " intreated to bear in mind, that if the members contend against the masters' interpetration, they will be contending for custom against a positive law ;" and the Report adds,—" In the opinion of the council, the Scale will not help us to claim 1s. per sheet for two notes in a volume. This is stated candidly and explicitly to you at the outset, that the trade council may be released from any odium hereafter of leading you into a contest for a charge which the Scale, taken by itself, cannot sanction." (p. 6.) Enough has been shown to convince all present that the law and practice are at variance with each other. Be it borne in mind, then, that neither ourselves nor the masters could alter that law. As we found it, so we were necessarily obliged to consider it. At once, then, we confess, that the words found in the Article " under the above proportion no charge to be made," were unanswerable ; for to say otherwise, would be to persist in making a charge in the face of the sentence declaring that " no charge" shall be made. In addition to this testimony, the Secretary of the Masters' Association read from a minute-book a decision given in July, 1805, but a short time after the Scale was made. This decision was signed by five masters whose names are appended to the 1805 Scale. It established the masters' interpretation, and showed beyond doubt that the practice which has prevailed is directly opposed to the decision given. It was a work of twenty-nine sheets, and had five notes. No man would think he was doing wrong, following up the custom of years, if he charged for these five notes one shilling per sheet, or twenty-nine shillings. " But," said five of the eight gentlemen who framed the Article itself in 1805, " neither number nor lines justify the charge ;" that is, there should be six, not five notes, or sixty lines of note, to warrant a charge throughout. We found it impossible to gainsay the meaning of this decision, or to prove that the practice of the trade was in accordance with the Article. But knowing how vastly important the trade deemed this bottom-note question, some inquiry was made into the effect of the alteration. From a promiscuous library 192 volumes were examined. The result showed that the cases are extremely rare in which the compositor will be a loser, for 186 had sufficient notes to constitute the charge ; three were without notes ; one had a single note ; and the other two might be called doubtful, the small type in them being explanations to wood-cuts. And if any man will look into a number of books, he will see that they are few indeed which, having notes, do not show two for each ten sheets they severally make. Cases of extraordinary sums paid were quoted; and were called iniquitous charges, paid to prevent disorder. One was a work of eighty-eight sheets; 4*l*. 8*s*. were paid for one note exceeding twenty lines, the difference in value of the note-matter over the text being about one shilling only. As it was in vain to follow up the subject, we determined upon obtaining a more liberal meaning to the actual wording than the resolution put before us gave. This we succeeded in, and we have no hesitation in stating that we believe a correct reading has now been arrived at. (See SCALE, p. 8.)

The arrangement made does not cause separate castings-up; a great error has been committed in supposing the principle ever implied such a trouble; for suppose the work makes thirty sheets, if the compositor cannot show six single notes (half lines or even words will do), or three notes, in themselves amounting to sixty lines, such as 18 in one, 30 in the second, and 12 in the third, no charge will be made for notes; but showing the number of notes, or notes having the requisite number of lines, the charge of one shilling per sheet will be made throughout. To simplify the present rule, the compositor must show two notes in every ten sheets, or one note averaging in every ten sheets twenty lines. This latter amendment upon the original intention will be found, in many instances, to be a saving clause for the trade; for though there may be works making twenty sheets which fall short of having four notes, yet, in such works, there may be two notes which added together make forty lines. In such a case, the compositor will still charge 20*s*. for placing notes, the value of which may be said to be but trifling. Where notes exceed the maximum quantities stated in the Article, such as more than four pages in every ten sheets in 4to or 8vo, the compositor will then charge 1*s*. 6*d*. per sheet, although the exact value of the notes may not be more than 1*s*. 2*d*.; and where 1*s*. 6*d*. will not pay, then the whole of the notes must be measured off, their value charged, and 1*s*. per sheet extra added to the cast-up for placing. A plan has been laid down for measuring off notes, quotations, or small type inserted in the text of a work, making more than one line, by adding to each note, quotation, &c., an extra line for the space which separates the small type from the text type. Every reference is to be considered a note, if only a word; and if a work be in pica and the notes in bourgeois, or three removes from the text, the compositor will only be called upon to compose the same number of thousands as though the notes were set in long primer, or two removes, which is decided to be the proper distinction for notes to all works. In cases where there are notes upon notes, quotations, &c., set up in smaller type than the notes, 1s. per sheet extra will be paid on every sheet where such small type is found. Extracts, &c., set up in a type between that used for the text and that for the notes, will also be paid 1s. per sheet extra where they occur; but if it can be shown that the intermediate type occurs in three-fourths of the work, that is, in fifteen sheets of a work making twenty sheets, then the compositor will charge 1s. per sheet for placing throughout. With regard to this charge for mixture of type, it was stated by the employers to be a charge unknown in years gone by; and was but another mode of adding to the price per 1000 for making up, which was included in Art. I.; that it had occasioned many of them great uneasiness in seeing a charge insisted upon of modern introduction, and though they had paid it, they had done so not as mixture of type, but looked upon works having it as occasioning additional trouble.

Art. XII.—*Vide* Scale, pp. 9-10.

Here was another equally difficult rule to determine, for the Article decides only a minimum charge, and this but for sizes down to 8vo. Side-notes to 12mo and smaller sized works, or when side-notes exceeded the average mentioned, how they were to be reckoned and charged is not stated, neither is a principle laid down which shall govern a charge for side-notes throughout. The employers have never recognised the system adopted by the trade of casting off side-notes, but have given a fixed sum per sheet instead. The Article will now be found complete. The minimum charge for side-notes to 12mo will be 2s.; 16mo, 18mo, and smaller sizes, 2s. 6d. per sheet. Upon all sizes for side-notes set in nonpareil, 6d. per sheet additional will be paid; if in pearl, 1s. per sheet. For casting off side-notes a simple rule has been devised. The compositor will ascertain the exact number of appearing lines, and multiply the number by 3; that is, twice for composition, and once for making-up or placing: and he will find that heavily side-noted works, by this system, will amply pay; while those less noted will give a charge, in most cases, equal to the present custom. Side-notes and cut-in notes will be paid throughout if occurring in one-fourth of the work, and not in distinct portions. Thus, in a work of twelve sheets, if side or cut-in notes are found in three out of the twelve sheets, the charge for such side or cut-in notes will be upon the whole twelve sheets; if occurring in less than one-fourth, they will then be paid on those sheets in which they appear. Double side-notes, or notes upon each side of the page, will be paid double the price specified for notes on one side of the page. As the trouble varies in respect to under-runners, or figures down the side of a page, it was deemed best that these should be left for settlement between the master and the journeymen.

Art. XIII.—*Vide* Scale, p. 10.

Greek, &c., exceeding three lines in any one sheet, will be paid 1*s.* additional to its value as cast up; the first three lines, entitling the charge of 1*s.*, being deducted.

Art. XIV.—*Vide* Scale, p. 11.

No addition has been made to this Art., it needing none. Alteration was not in the power of the Conference, otherwise no doubt it would have been attempted; the employers observing, " that the price of Greek without accents was extravagant, as the compositor could set plain Greek in almost the same time he could foreign matter."

Art. XV.—*Vide* Scale, p. 11.

Upon the subject of Hebrew much discussion took place; it being contended that the Art. could not be adhered to by London masters. It was said, too, that Greek and Hebrew works would be done in Germany, where wages were very low. The employers wished us to admit of a mutual settlement with respect to this kind of work, so that they might give to a compositor a certain price per sheet. This we objected to, as it allowed one man to have an advantage over his fellow-man, he being willing to take a less price than his neighbour. The employers said they could always have it done on the establishment; this we admitted, but added that that was a recognised system of working; whereas the other mode would be setting men in competition with each other. The rule was passed without addition.

Art. XVI.—*Vide* Scale, p. 11.

Here we had an imperfect rule, and but indefinite means to alter it. The Article is silent upon music which has no sonnet type, such as instrumental music. It was therefore inapplicable as a rule. The modern founts of music are very different to those formerly in use, and vary in thickness as well as mode of casting. No price could be settled upon to meet the whole of these founts, so it was agreed that music should be paid by agreement between the employer and employed ; that is, the latter, if on an entire work, should get as much per week as their services are worth ; and if setting up a few pages only, make such a charge as will pay them for their labour, and be just to the employer.

ART. XVII.—*Vide* SCALE, p. 11.

This Art. has not been added to ; the *2s.* given for index matter per sheet being said to be good evidence of its being entitled to be cast up as distinct from the work. It was agreed, however, that column-matter, in indexes, should be charged the usual extra for.

ART. XVIII.—*Vide* SCALE, p. 11.

This Article applies to booksellers' catalogues only. "Not in-cluding the numbering" means, that when the compositor has to supply or correct the numbers used in a bookseller's catalogue, an extra charge shall be made equivalent to the lost time occasioned. The words "in whatever language" mean those in which common type is used.

ART. XIX.—*Vide* SCALE, p. 12.

A long and animated discussion followed the reading of this Ar-ticle, the employers wishing to be consulted in all chapel regulations respecting hours of work, commencing and ending ; and mentioned the various interruptions their businesses were subjected to by cha-pels, &c. What they wanted was, that before any regulation was made, their consent should be obtained, ere it was adopted. A reso-lution framed in accordance thereto was proposed. This we resisted, and said that chapels were a protection rather than an injury to employers. Some restriction was absolutely necessary, as many men would work in their meal times and at extraordinary hours, if per-mitted, occasioning distrust and jealousy. Men were always anxious to fulfil, to the letter, the instructions of the overseer both as to coming early or working late ; and chapels, after all, did but keep in order the refractory, when, but for them, disputes amongst the members would often be endless. Such a resolution, we stated, if allowed to be printed, would be discreditable to those we served. The employers ultimately consented to withdraw it. The Article remains as before.

Art. XX.—*Vide* Scale, p. 12.

This Article excepts auctioneers' work, leaving it to be inferred that auctioneers' catalogues and particulars should be charged according to Art. I. We spoke of the labour this work often occasioned, and it was decided that it should be paid an uniform price of 6*d*. per 1000, leaded or solid. Under this Art. came a description of work called one-sheet tracts, always in dispute, and generally composed by boys. The employers, it was said, could not pay them as jobs—they were never intended so to be considered. The letter, leads, white-lines, and furniture, were always the same; and to jump from 5*d*. to 7*d*. per 1000 for a reprint leaded tract was too great to be allowed. These tracts seemed to us much to resemble one-sheet publications; and being sensible of the difference which this work presented from ordinary jobs, as also that journeymen seldom obtained them, but boys were kept constantly going even to an unnecessary, and on the part of the employers not desired, increase of their numbers, we consented to view these sheet-tracts as though they were publications; that is, allowing them to be cast up according to Art. I., adding to the cast up 2*s*. 6*d*., which is equivalent to $\frac{3}{4}d$., and sometimes 1*d*. extra per 1000, the only real difference being to the compositor that he will deduct for reprint and leads; but a manuscript tract set in small pica will be found, by adding the 2*s*. 6*d*., to be close upon 7*d*. per thousand, and a reprint one equal to the ordinary price of manuscript. By this addition we settled a long-disputed description of work, we believe to the benefit of journeymen generally. Jobs partaking of the character of book-work will be cast up in sheets, and take the usual extras for notes, column-work, &c., as stated in the Scale.

Art. XXI.—*Vide* Scale, pp. 12-13.

The following words were allowed to be added to this Art., because, by resorting to a different scheme of imposition, the same result could be obtained ; and as we all along wished to procure for the piece-hands works which have hitherto been done by boys or on the establishment, but little harm could be done by agreeing that " works printed on alternate pages only, the blank at the back of each page not to be charged."

Art. XXII.—*Vide* Scale, p. 13.

Leases, deeds, and charter-parties, here called broadsides, evidently mean undisplayed matter set up at a great width, occasioning infinite trouble in the composition. The Article means, then, broadsides set in

B

one measure, in which case it pays, above the dimensions of crown, double price. When, however, undisplayed broadsides are set up in two, three, or four columns, one-fourth the price of common matter extra will be paid; if in five columns, one half; if in six columns, or more, double the price of common matter.

The Scale makes no provision for displayed broadsides. A price has, however, been put upon these, for which see Scale, p. 13.

Arts. XXIII., XXIV., and XXV., finishing the 1805-10 Scale, remain without addition.—*Vide* Scale, p. 13.

Having thus gone through the Scale, we come to what is called a rider to the Scale, which at the will of twenty masters took off one-eighth of the price per 1000 allowed in 1810 upon Art. I., which Article is said to have been mutually agreed to by masters and men in 1805, and therefore, in justice, ought only to have been altered with the approval of the men. It relates to reprint; and is an ever-memorable instance of the condition of the trade in and out of society. We approached this 1816 modification with much concern; indeed, we repudiated its authority to be ranked as part of the Scale, from the fact of its being a rule of the masters' own creation. Having, at some length, pointed out the losses the trade experienced from this excessive reduction, and the extraordinary definitions given to the word "reprints" by several masters, we sought for an advance of $\frac{1}{4}d.$ per thousand upon plain reprints, and an understanding of the term itself. The masters seemed prepared for this attempt, and met our proposition by a counter one: viz., "That in consequence of the great facility of communication now existing between all parts of the kingdom, and the low rate of wages paid in many places, it is not advisable, for either masters or men, to add any inducement to the removal of reprints from London by advancing the price per 1000." The employers added, "They would feel a pleasure in granting the advance sought, but such was the effect of provincial competition, that to increase the price of reprints would be to lose them entirely to London." Cases were given even under the present mode of payment. One gentleman said, a work of fourteen or fifteen vols. was lost to the London business and had gone to Oxford, because the London masters could not do the work so low as it was agreed to be taken for. Other gentlemen observed, that they had lost works in a like manner; and one employer stated, that he had estimated for some volumes that had gone to Bungay, in Suffolk, though his compositors were walking about for want of employment. The employers generally said, that we would be best consulting the interest of the trade if we did not further persist in this matter, as it would only tend to increase apprentices, and lead to other improper measures being resorted to, to get this kind of work out of the respectable offices where journeymen were employed. Met by such experience as the foregoing, we set about obtaining something like a distinct understanding in regard to what was and what was not a reprint. After considerable difficulty, the conference succeeded in settling what may be called four kinds of reprints. There may be said to be: 1. Reprints composed from print copy, unaltered by the author or corrector, and not derived from various sources ; for such works $\frac{3}{4}d.$ per 1000 will have to be deducted. 2. Reprints having manuscript alterations ; for such $\frac{1}{2}d.$ per 1000 will have to be deducted. 3. Reprints consisting of half manuscript and half reprint ; these will be paid as manuscript. And 4. Reprints having manuscript insertions numerously interspersed throughout the work, although amounting, when reckoned together, to but one-fourth, or even less, of the work ; these will also be paid as manuscript. We conclude our notice of this much-disputed question, by saying, that our right to an advance upon plain reprint was admitted, but its effect was so much questioned, as to render it dangerous to grant it.

The next heading in the new Scale, under the title of " Addenda," is Appeal Cases. It may be naturally supposed that if the masters anticipated our attack upon reprints, we certainly ought not to be alarmed if we heard from them of reduction upon Appeal Cases. We doubt not that the majority of the trade expect to hear that this reduction has been agreed to by us ; and perhaps not alone upon the price per thousand, but also the usual, but disputed charge, for sidenotes. Now this payment of 8d. per 1000 for Appeal Cases has ever been objected to by certain employers. In many offices establishment hands and boys have engrossed this work ; and even when piece hands have done it in these offices, the money has been indirectly paid. The masters frankly said they never would admit the charge, because no authority nor labour could be shown for the demand made. They also said, in answer to a statement made by us that those who had Appeal Cases done could afford to pay the extra 1d. per 1000, that there was as much competition going on and estimates given for this work as any other. Well, we had two important charges to struggle for in settling the price of Appeal Cases ; and looking at the position of the trade, and always wishing to destroy any incentive for boys being taken, we held it advisable to yield a little to secure the remainder. And we think that when the alteration is calmly considered, and Rule XXII. of the Scale read, which gives a higher price for an increased measure, the trade will be satisfied with our arrangement. First, as to the price per 1000. By limiting the dimensions of this work, we still preserve the old price of 8*d*. per 1000; that is, where the compositor has to set up Appeal Cases exceeding 40 ems pica wide, 8*d*. per 1000 will be charged; 40 ems, and under, 7*d*. per 1000. The noted M'Dowall case was 42 ems pica wide; so that, after all, 8*d*. per 1000 would be paid for it if again done. This being settled, the masters said piece hands would in future have this work to do. Then we come to side-notes. At the time of the strike, the masters said these side-notes should be charged according to the Book-scale; which would give about 1*s*. or 1*s*. 6*d*. per sheet. However, no such price was mooted to us, and we have the satisfaction of saying that side-notes to Appeal Cases will be paid, if a broad, 3*s*.; double narrow, 5*s*.; double broad, 6*s*. per sheet, or 4pp. folio.

COLUMN-WORK.—A distinction has been made between column-work and tabular and table-work; and column-matter, as distinguished from table and tabular, is matter made up continuously in two or more columns, not dependent upon each other for their arrangement; that is, matter running from the first column into the second, and so on, such as ordinary two-column matter. In 4to and 8vo, 1*s*. per sheet for two columns will be charged. Need we say that, at present, no more would be charged for 12mo and 16mo? But, in future, 12mo will be paid 1*s*. 6*d*.; 16mo and smaller sizes, 2*s*. per sheet. The employers laid before us specimens of column-work which admitted of no charge for columns in measures above 17 ems in width of the type used. This was so different to our views, that we at once said such a proposition could not be entertained; for in nonpareil, if the measure were nine ems pica wide, no charge for columns was proposed to be made. By practically showing the difficulties belonging to column-work, we succeeded not only in obtaining the advance mentioned upon 12mo and 16mo, but also the prices clearly stated in the Scale to be paid for column-matter, p. 15.

The next is Tabular and Table-work. Table and tabular-work is matter set up in three or more columns depending upon each other, and reading across the page. (See pp. 16 and 17, SCALE.)

Wrappers will be paid as settled in 1839, an addition being made to the resolutions then passed, affecting advertisements in the body of weekly publications, such as the London Journal, &c. These will be paid in the same way as occurring in advertisement sheets ; when a whole page is standing, it is the property of the master ; when less than a page, the property of the men.

Under the head "Miscellaneous," will be found many important methods of charging what may be called additions to works, and matter beyond the ordinary character. Prefatory matter, which includes Prefaces, Contents, Preliminary Dissertations, Biographical Memoirs, &c., making a sheet, or under, set up in larger type than, or the same size as, the body of the text, to be paid as pages of the work ; if in smaller type, to be cast up according to their bodies, the extras of the work being added to the cast-up. But when either of the above-named exceeds a sheet, then it must be regarded as appendix matter. (See p. 18.)

"All works to be cast up as sent to press." This sentence gave rise to considerable discussion ; the employers wishing works to be cast up as first sent out. This we opposed firmly ; for no limit could be placed upon the extent the compositor would be thus injured. All wood-cuts inserted in proofs, chapters made pages, and so on, would be lost to the compositor. After several sittings, we heard that our objections had prevailed ; but to suit cases that may demand a casting up, in conse-quence of great delay, or even the work not going to press, another sentence has been added, so that the rule will read, "All works to be cast up as sent to press, except by mutual agreement between employer and employed."

Slip-matter, which has become so frequent now-a-days, was wished to be cast-up at an advanced price of $\frac{1}{2}d.$ per 1000, as sent out in slips. This was even less than the 2s. 6d. given upon publications. The pro-position was declined acceptance. Considering, however, the difference to the compositor of first making up his matter, and from sending it out in slips, in justice to the employers we agreed to the following modifi-cations :—Works in two or three columns, sent out in single columns, to abandon the column charge, providing each column exceeds 12 ems pica wide ; the extras given by Art. IX. upon long primer and smaller type, for 16mo, 18mo, &c., to be relinquished ; and matter sent out without head-lines, the value of the head-lines to be deducted.

Thus, as the compositor has not to make up columns above 12 ems pica wide, or make up his pages in a 16mo or 18mo forme at his own expense, or to set the head-lines to his matter when first sent out, it seemed proper to admit of these trifling reductions. In deducting for head-lines, the compositor should cast up his work in the usual way, *i.e.* inclusive of the head-line; and then ascertaining, say in 8vo, the exact value of sixteen solid lines, deduct it from the actual cast-up of the sheet. Example: price per sheet, by letters, 19s. 10d.; deduct value of sixteen head-lines, 6d.; price per sheet, 19s. 4d., which is 19s. 6d. Before dismissing the modifications connected with slip-matter, the compositor should particularly observe, that if he be on a work in columns 12 ems pica or less wide; or the work be set in small pica or larger type; or the work be made up in pages with a folio or any head line, yet sent out in a slip form; the reductions mentioned will not have to be made, as the regulation only applies to " works sent out in slips *not* made up into perfect pages."

The rule respecting woodcuts (p. 19) was made in order that the piece hand might get the composition of these advantageous works. It will be noticed it is the woodcuts, not the matter, which is to be mutually settled; and this only where they exceed a fourth of the work; thus insuring the piece hand a charge of one-fourth for wood-cuts; and if the trouble requires a higher charge, the sum to be arranged between the master and the men.

The Scale, with the additions, definitions, and explanations settled by the Committee of Conference, comes into operation on the 1st December, 1847, and will be applicable to all descriptions of work mentioned therein commenced on or after that date.

To the Scale as printed, a valuable Abstract has been prepared. It shows at a glance the price per 1000 for all founts down to diamond for leaded and solid matter, whether manuscript or reprint, common or foreign; also for English, English and foreign, and foreign diction-aries; English, English and foreign, and foreign grammars; Greek with and without accents. It tells you what to add upon reprints having manuscript insertions, as also for stereotype matter with high and low spaces; minimum and maximum quantities of notes. A copious Index is also added, which mentions in various ways the references to charges upon all kinds and peculiarities of work. We have by us voluminous notes, now collected together, and forming a minute-book of the proceedings of the Conference, which gives the substance of nearly every observation made, and who made it, whether masters or men, more particularly the latter. By it, at any future time, the reasons given and the meaning intended upon the different features of the Scale, may be at once learned. Had such a book been handed down from 1805, many of those disputes upon words, and canvassings of the intentions of those who met so long since, must necessarily have been prevented. The expense of this portion of the Conference may be described as follows :—

	£	s.	d.
Lost time of seven* persons, at 6s. per day, seventeen days....	35	14	0
Expenses incurred by the eight persons, both before and after each sitting, 2s. per day being allowed	13	12	0
Cost of refreshment for meetings beyond the seventeen above-mentioned, and for which time has not been paid......	4	9	0
Lost time paid trade committee and the seven* persons forming the arbitration committee, assembled together mutually to discuss the several points in the Green-book, two day sittings	7	4	0
	£60	19	0

The employers, besides having given so much valuable time, must have gone to great expense, as the Conference was held in the best rooms of the Freemasons' Tavern, Great Queen Street, two rooms being specially engaged. It is impossible to speak too highly of the kind and gentlemanly bearing shown us by those whom we had to meet. From first to last we experienced this kindness; it never abated; and we always found a listening ear extended to what we had to say.

But a few words more, and this Report is ended. It cannot be supposed that this meeting can properly estimate the work as now performed. Time alone will prove this. In the speedy settlement of his cast-up, the assurance that his foundation for making a charge is good, the hours he will save by having definite rules to direct him, the compositor will, as weeks roll on, appreciate the amended Scale. As part concoctors of it, we are well satisfied with it, and believe that if we had to perform the same duties again, they would not be so advantageously settled upon the part of the journeymen. Would that

---

* The secretary formed the eighth member. As his time is allowed for in his salary, no payment was made to him for lost time.

every member of the trade had experienced what we have during the last few months, and not one of them, we feel convinced, would remain aloof from the Society. The trade owes all it has to the union which has prevailed ; and, whilst it is preserved, we may rest assured of the Scale being held inviolable. There are two essential reasons why the trade should be united : 1, because the charges in the Scale are by this means uniformly adhered to; and 2, because the respectable master (he who employs journeymen with but a limited number of boys) is supported in consequence, as the Society will not allow the principles of the Scale to be broken; employers generally, so far as our wages are concerned, are thereby induced to pay according to the rules laid down. The same cause which should actuate us is acknowledged by them. We wish to receive uniform wages, they wish all masters to pay the same; consequently, while we uphold a society, we do infinite service to our employers. It is from practical experience we speak ; and as such we trust it will be received. With you we desire present prices to be continued. For this to be, we must all act together; nothing short of union will suffice. We trust, the result of our labours, as now before you, may prove satisfactory; we have done our best without exception. And should it be found, as practice is brought to bear upon the new rules, that their explicitness will prevent unpleasantness in offices with respect to charges, and lead to our working together more harmoniously than before, then we shall feel gratified at having accomplished so great an improvement. Appreciating the confidence you reposed in us, we fervently hope that you will find it has not been abused; and subscribe ourselves, your most obedient servants,

THE JOURNEYMEN MEMBERS OF THE ARBITRATION COMMITTEE,

WILLIAM DREW,	ROBERT CHAPMAN,
G. E. ADCOCK,	FRANCIS FELTOE,
JOHN FERGUSON,	WILLIAM CRAIG,
LEWIS MILLER,	EDWARD EDWARDS.

NOTE.—As the mutually agreed-to Scale does not speak of News or Parliamentary Work, the Scale of the former, as printed on p. 55, and that of the latter, printed on p. 67 of the London Union edition of the Compositors' Scale, are appended to this Report for the guidance of the trade. The employers at the conference observed, that "they did not intend to discuss the prices paid for newspapers;" and with respect to Parliamentary work, they added, that "as this kind of work affected but few offices, it was unnecessary to interfere with the regulations upon which the same was at present charged."

APPENDIX.

SCALE FOR NEWS WORK.

	Per Week.		Per Galley.		Per Hour
Morning Papers	£2 8 0	—	3s. 10d.	—	11½d.
Evening Papers	£2 3 6	—	3s. 7d.	—	10½d.

The charge of tenpence-halfpenny per hour refers solely to employment upon time ; every odd quarter of a galley, on quantity, must carry the charge of 11d.; as the charge of 10½d. would bring down the galley to 3s. 6d.; which is contrary to the scale.

Assistants on other journals are paid the same as Evening Papers ; the Sunday Papers, having their galleys of various lengths, are paid at the rate of 8½d. per 1000, or 10d. per hour.

The only meaning that can be gathered from the first part of this article is, that papers which are published twice or three times a week, are paid the same as Evening Papers. With respect to the second part, the price per thousand for a Sunday or Weekly Paper is the same, but time-work is paid only 10d. per hour.

Long primer and minion galleys, cast as nigh 5000 letters as possible, (at present varying from that number to 5200, partly arising from a variation in the founders' standard,) are, per 1000, on

		Morning.		Evening.
Long Primer and Minion	-	9d.	-	8½d.
Nonpariel	- - - -	10d.	-	9½d.
Pearl	- - - -	11d.	-	10½d.

Or a reduction, in proportion to value, on the galley quantity.

This article has been greatly misunderstood ; it has been supposed to contain a licence for the news compositor to set up 5200 letters for a galley, but it does not *say* any such thing ; it simply states the fact, that at the period when the Scale was framed, some galleys contained more than 5000 letters. As the price per thousand is clearly established, the compositor should set up neither more nor less than just such a number of lines as will amount to 4s. 10d. on a Morning Paper, or 3s. 7d. on an Evening Paper. 3

The galley on Morning Papers consists of 120 lines long primer, and 40 *after-lines*—minion 88, and 30 *after-lines*—on papers 22 ems long primer wide ; other widths in proportion ; and a *finish* of five hours. Another *mode* is, one galley, and a *finish* of six hours. Twelve hours on and twelve off (including refreshment time) was the original agreement.

c

The galley on Morning Papers consists of 120 lines long primer, and 40 after-lines ; which amounts to just this, that it consists of a galley and a quarter and ten lines (long primer) ; that the workman shall compose 7040 letters for 3s. 10d., instead of receiving his just reward, 5s. 3½d. ; and that the full hand on his first work is paid at the rate of 6½d. per thousand, though the Scale gives him 9d.

There is also a mis-statement in respect to the length of the galley ; for it will be found that on casting up a galley of the length and width given, it would contain 5280 letters, thus exceeding the legal quantity by 280 letters, and being a direct variance with the first part of the Scale, which directs that "long primer and minion galleys are to be cast as nigh 5000 letters as possible." The *first* direction is that which is really meant to be adopted, and which the remaining regulations of the Scale alone sanction.

With regard to after-lines upon the first work on Morning Papers, we find that the custom existed as far back as the year 1770, but no reason for the practice can be assigned, though it is understood to have been adopted to lighten or to leave nothing to compose for the finish, and thus enable the compositors to go early to their beds ; an advantage which, from the complete alteration in the nature of Morning Papers, it is totally impossible they can now enjoy.

By a finish of five hours on Morning, and six hours on Evening Papers, it was not meant that the compositors should produce five or six quarters of a galley, as that would produce considerably more than they were paid for ; but from the best information that can now be obtained of the nature of newspapers at the time this mode of work was introduced, it appears that the *first work and after-lines* of the full hands and the *galley* of the supernumeraries were sufficient to produce the paper, and that the "finish" was merely waiting to see whether any news of importance should arrive, (during which time they might put in letter for the next day,) and assisting to put the paper to press.

The *time* of beginning to be the same uniformly, as agreed upon by the printer and companionship, i. e. either a two, three, or four o'clock paper—and at whatever hour the journal goes to press one morning regulates the hour of commencing work for the next day's publication, provided it should be over the hour originally agreed upon—if under, the time is in the compositor's favour. The hour of commencing work on Sunday is regulated by the time of finishing on Saturday morning.

This article it is impossible to understand ; but the general practice appears to be, when the paper goes to press two or three hours after the specified time, to take off one, and sometimes two, quarters from the first work of the next day ; but generally commencing at the time originally agreed upon on a Sunday, making each week's work complete in itself.

Ten hours' composition is the specified time for Evening Papers—all composition to cease when the day's publication goes to press ; any work required afterwards to be paid for extra or deducted from the first work of the next publication. This does not apply to *second editions ;* those being connected solely with the antecedent paper, must be paid for extra.

Matter set up for a Morning Paper is invariably paid Morning Paper price, although such matter is set up in London, and the paper is published in the provinces.

Newspapers in a foreign language take, of course, the same advance as is allowed on book-work.

A system termed *finishing* having been formerly introduced, it is necessary to state that no mode of working can be considered fair (except as before stated) otherwise than by the galley or hour.

No apprentices to be employed on daily papers.

Apprentices are not permitted to work on *daily* papers, whether stamped or unstamped.

Compositors on weekly papers, if engaged on the establishment, to receive not less than 36s. per week ; and if employed on time, to charge one hour for every portion of an hour.

Compositors called in to assist on weekly papers are entitled to charge not less than two hours if employed on time, or less than half a galley if paid by lines; and persons regularly employed in a house where a weekly paper is done, if required to leave their ordinary work to assist on the paper, are entitled to not less than a quarter of a galley or an hour for each time of being called on.

The method of charging column work upon newspapers is as follows : half measure is charged one-third more, third measure is charged one-half, and four column measure is charged double.

One-fourth is allowed for distribution on weekly papers, when more than one galley has been composed; but if less than a galley, no deduction is made.

SCALE FOR PARLIAMENTARY WORK.

1. That all work for either House of Parliament, such as Reports, Minutes of Evidence, &c., as well as Reports of Royal Commissions of Inquiry, whether manuscript or reprint, leaded or solid, to be charged at 6½d. per 1000, including English and brevier ; and always to be cast up according to the type in which it is composed. Tables to be charged 1s. 1d. per thousand.

2. That all works not intended for either House of Parliament, but executed for the Public Departments, to be paid according to the Scale for book-work, with all the extras.

3. That Private Parliamentary Bills be charged 7d. per thousand, and table-matter in them at 1s. 2d. per thousand.

This article does not interfere with those bills in parliament which are of the *regular* size, and for which a stated price is paid. (See page 19, Book Scale.)

4. That pica or any other type as a standard is in opposition to the practice of the business, and in no case to be admitted ; but all Reports, Minutes of Evidence, Accounts, Appendices, &c., are to be cast up according to the type in which they are composed.

5. That pages consisting of two or three columns with one or more headings, or three or four columns without headings, to be charged as tabular, or one and one-half common matter.

6. That pages consisting of four or more columns, with one or more headings, or five or more columns without headings, to be charged as table, or double the price of common matter.

7. That when short pages occur in a series of tables, to be

charged as full pages; but where a table or piece of table occurs in a Report, &c., to be charged only the depth of the table, measuring from the head to the conclusion of the table. The same rule to apply to tabular.

In a *series* of tables all *pieces* of pages left blank are charged as table; in jobs or works consisting of plain matter,where tables or tabular matter are introduced, whatever blank occurs is considered as common matter; unless the table or tabular matter forms more than three-fourths of a page; in which latter case, the page is charged as a full page table or tabular as the case may be.

8. That all headings to table or tabular matter, when in smaller type than the body of the table, to be charged extra.

9. Pages consisting of four or five blank columns to be charged tabular; but when the columns are six or more, to be charged table, cast up to the size of the type used in the Reports or Bills in which they occur.

10. When blank forms are used by themselves, detached from any Bill, &c., to be charged as pica table or tabular, according to the number of the columns, as specified in Resolution IX.

11. Plain matter divided into two columns to be charged not less than 1s. per sheet.

12. All read-over pages (as in Dr. and Cr. accounts of two pages) where one page only is tabular or table, the same charge to be made for both pages, and in no case shall read-over pages be charged less than tabular.

13. Side-notes of "broad quotations," and not exceeding five lines per page, in quartos and folios, to be charged 1s. 6d. per sheet; in "double narrows," not exceeding five lines per page, 2s. per sheet, throughout such Report, Appendix, &c., excepting when pages comprising the whole width of the page (including the space for side-notes) shall occur; all above that proportion to be paid *ad valorem*. Where double side-notes occur in a page, to be charged double the above sum.

Reports, Minutes of Evidence, and Appendices, are all cast up separately, and take only the extras which strictly belong to them. Thus, if a Report, &c. have side notes, and the Appendix is without side notes, no charge is made on the Appendix for side notes.

14. Where two bottom notes, or one note of twenty lines, occur in a Report, Bill, Appendix, &c. ; a charge of 1s. per sheet to be made throughout such Report, Bill, Appendix, &c.; all above, to be charged according to their value.

N.B.—The foregoing Regulations are applicable solely to Parliamentary Work.

Catchpool, Printer, 5, St. John's Square, Clerkenwell.

British Labour Struggles:
Contemporary Pamphlets 1727-1850

An Arno Press/New York Times Collection